School Literacy Skills

D1581048

Comprehension

Ages 5-7

PHOTOCOPIABLE SKILLS ACTIVITIES

Author	Helena Rigby	Series designer	Lynda Murray
Editor	Clare Gallaher	Illustrations	Julie Clough
Assistant editor	Dulcie Booth	Cover artwork	Joy Monkhouse

Published by Scholastic Ltd
Villiers House
Clarendon Avenue
Leamington Spa
Warwickshire CV32 5PR

Text © Helena Rigby 2001
© 2001 Scholastic Ltd

Printed by Bell & Bain Ltd, Glasgow

67890   567890

British Library Cataloguing-in-Publication Data
A catalogue record for this book is available from the British Library.

ISBN 0-439-01914-1

Acknowledgments

The publishers would like to thank the following for permission to reproduce copyright material.

Egmont Children's Books Ltd for the use of 'A Hibernating Hedgehog' from *Animal Nonsense Rhymes* by Martin Honeysett © 1984, Martin Honeysett (1984, Methuen Children's Books, an imprint of Egmont Children's Books Ltd).

Richard Gilbert for the use of 'Acorn Bill' by Ruth Ainsworth from *All Different* © 1947, Ruth Ainsworth (1947, Heinemann).

David Higham Associates for the use of 'The Quarrel' from *Silver Sand and Snow* by Eleanor Farjeon © 1951, Eleanor Farjeon (1951, Michael Joseph).

David Higham Associates for the use of 'The beech tree' from *Oh Really Rabbit!* by Ruth Manning-Sanders © 1985, Ruth Manning-Sanders (1985, Associated Book Publishers).

Sarah Matthews as Literary Executrix of the Estate of Stanley Cook for the use of 'The Gerbil' from *Come Along* by Stanley Cook © Stanley Cook.

David Mostyn for the use of original illustrations on page 128 © 2001, David Mostyn, previously unpublished.

Penguin Books Ltd for the use of an extract from 'Geraldine gets lucky' by Robert Leeson which originally appeared as 'The frog who went a-wooing' in *Puffin Flight* magazine © 1995, Robert Leeson (1985, Hamish Hamilton).

Penguin Books Ltd for the use of an extract from *Finders Keepers* by June Crebbin © 1989, June Crebbin (1989, Kestrel).

Penguin Books Ltd for the use of an extract from *Captain Daylight and the Big Hold-up* by David Mostyn © 1994, David Mostyn (1994, Puffin).

The Peters Fraser and Dunlop Group Ltd for the use of 'If I had a silver coin' by Wendy Cope, originally entitled 'If I had a ten pence piece' from *Twiddling Your Thumbs: Hand Rhymes* © 1992, Wendy Cope (1992, Faber & Faber).

The Random House Group Ltd for the use of 'Ask Mummy, ask Daddy' from *I Din' Do Nuttin'* by John Agard © 1991, John Agard (1991, Bodley Head).

Marian Reiner, Literary Agent, New York for the use of 'Hideout' from *In the Woods, In the Meadow, In the Sky* by Aileen Fisher © 1965, Aileen Fisher © renewed 1993, Aileen Fisher (1965, Scribner).

John Rice for the use of 'Monkey Tricks' from *Bears Don't Like Bananas* by John Rice © 1991, John Rice (1991, Macdonald Young Books).

Stainer and Bell Ltd for the use of 'Little Arabella Miller' by Ann Elliott from *Fingers and Thumbs* © 1933, Stainer and Bell Ltd.

Celia Warren for the use of 'Spider's Song' by Celia Warren from *First Verses* by John Foster and Carol Thompson © 1996, Celia Warren (1996, Oxford University Press).

Clive Webster for the use of 'When I get up in the morning' by Clive Webster from *First Verses* by John Foster and Carol Thompson © 1996, Clive Webster (1996, Clive Webster).

Every effort has been made to trace copyright holders and the publishers apologise for any inadvertent omissions.

Contents

Section ① (5-year-olds)

Section ② (6-year-olds)

Section ② *contd*

Drama

Section ③ (7-year-olds)

Poetry

Fiction

Section ③ *contd*

Non-fiction

Drama

Introduction

Comprehension means 'understanding' and, in its narrowest sense, comprehension material tests children's understanding of what they read. However, true 'comprehension' goes much deeper than this, and therefore the main objective of the *Scholastic Literacy Skills: Comprehension* series is to foster reading and comprehension skills in the widest possible sense, so that children not only learn how to read, and extract information from a variety of types of text, but also begin to appreciate the enjoyment and learning they can gain from a range of material. While the children are working on the texts in these books, they will become more aware of the different features of various types of text genres, and will begin to understand how organisation of language, choice of vocabulary, grammar, layout and presentation all influence meaning.

WORKING AT TEXT LEVEL

Scholastic Literacy Skills: Comprehension Ages 5–7 gives children the opportunity to develop work at text level. This provides the essential context for work at sentence and word levels. Text level work is also a vital part of the meaning-making process which is at the root of effective reading. Care has been taken to ensure that the content of the texts is compatible with the range required by the National Literacy Strategy *Framework for Teaching*.

The book is divided into three sections. This structure is designed to develop, through progression, the skills children will need to:
- identify main points
- be aware of the organisation and linguistic features of different text genres
- be aware of the differences between fact, opinion and persuasion
- develop an awareness of tense, mood and person in writing and how they affect meaning.

READING STRATEGIES

In order to learn to read well, a reader must be motivated. The variety of reading material offered by the units in this book will ensure the children's interest will be captured so that their reading confidence and experience will be developed.

Testing comprehension can never be a precise art. Any reader brings to a new text a considerable 'baggage' of opinions, knowledge (or lack of it), personal experience and expectations. All these factors are bound to affect how that person responds to what they are reading and how much, or what type of, information they will retrieve from it.

To be able to understand a text fully, a reader will ultimately need to have acquired the skills of detailed (close) reading, and search reading (including skimming and scanning). To answer questions on the content of the text, the reader will require retrieval skills to locate and select the appropriate information, as well as communication skills to express responses verbally or in writing. These are all sophisticated skills that experienced readers have generally developed. However, they can be engendered in the naive and inexperienced reader by question and answer and by presenting the learner with appropriate material to foster reading development.

Close reading

Reading a text in detail gives the reader a clear understanding of what it contains. The passage should usually be read more than once, particularly if the content or subject matter is difficult or unfamiliar. Additionally, inexperienced readers will benefit from the text being discussed to alert them to the different points raised. This initial read through and discussion should allow the reader to fully grasp the meaning and intent of the author. Reading is an active skill and it constantly involves guessing, predicting, checking and asking oneself questions as the text is read. This should be developed and capitalised on when discussing possible responses to comprehension questions.

Skimming and scanning

Once the reader is familiar with the text and understands it, search skills are required if the information needed to respond to a particular question is to be located swiftly. The reader needs to be able to skim through the passage quickly and scan the parts of the text where the answer might lie. Identifying the key words in a question will help to locate the information needed in the text for the response.

Answering the questions

Answering comprehension questions can be challenging for a young reader, particularly in the early stages of reading development. It would be of value to the children if the texts, and possible answers to the questions, could be discussed in small groups before they are asked to work individually. The children could be shown strategies for locating the information they need for the answer. This will help them to structure their answers and will also support any children who have limited reading and writing skills. Where appropriate, children should be encouraged to give written answers in complete sentences, and this will also enhance their writing skills.

TYPES OF QUESTION

The emphasis of the work in the units in this book is on a range of comprehension skills developed through sentence structures and language appropriate for the target age groups. The four aspects of comprehension covered by the questions for each of the units are literal, inferential, deductive and evaluative. Each of these tests a different facet of the reader's understanding of the texts. Explanations of these four types are given below, but it should be recognised that there is a considerable amount of overlap and that questions may sometimes fall between two or more categories.

● **Literal comprehension** centres on ideas and information that are quite explicit in a particular text. The reader is required to locate the response to a question, the clues to which lie on the surface of the text. In its simplest form, literal comprehension can be the recognition or recall of a single fact or incident, but it can also take more complex forms, such as the recognition or recall of a series of facts or the sequencing of incidents. For example, to sequence events, the children will need to be able to identify sequential clues in the text which will relate one element to another and predict the order.

● **Inferential comprehension** requires the reader to do some detective work and 'read between the lines' by finding meanings that are not directly explained. The information needed to respond to an inferential question is implicit in the text, and the reader needs to make inferences based on what has been read to formulate an answer. This type of question is more challenging, particularly for inexperienced readers, as it explores the extent to which the reader is aware of the nuances of meaning in the text. Children may, initially, need help to look for hidden clues and to link cause and effect.

● **Deductive comprehension** demands that the reader delves even deeper into the passage to make inferences based, not only on the text, but also on the reader's own experience and background knowledge. The reader is required to draw on personal knowledge and demonstrate a broader understanding of the text using links of cause and effect drawn from experience. Again, children may need support and guidance in formulating their answers, particularly in the early stages.

● **Evaluative comprehension** asks the reader to make an evaluation of arguments or ideas suggested by the text. In order to do this, readers need to compare the information provided with their own experiences, knowledge or values. Answers given to this type of question depend on readers' assessment of a situation and how they would react to it, given their own inclinations and experiences. Generally, it is not possible to provide set answers to these questions, although pointers to the areas that should be covered are sometimes offered.

ABOUT THE UNITS

The activities in the units unite the skills of reading and writing. They also involve speaking and listening as the work is discussed with the children before they make a written response. Each unit comprises a reading activity and questions that focus on the four types of comprehension described above. The units cover a variety and balance of eight different fiction and non-fiction genres, and the activities are arranged in groups by genre. (The genre of each passage is indicated at the top of each page.) The eight text genres are:

● poetry   *Non-fiction* ● report
● fiction   ● recount
● drama   ● explanation
                ● instructions
                ● discussion

Each unit follows the same pattern: a reading passage is followed by comprehension questions based on the text. The passages gradually increase in length and difficulty across each section, with each section targeting a particular age group. This progression is achieved by the text using appropriate language and sentence structures for the age group, the questions increasing in number and the type of questions becoming more challenging.

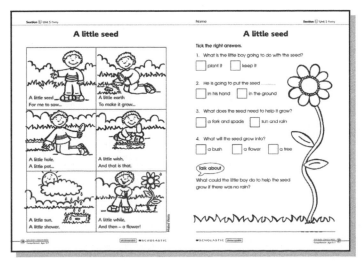

ABOUT THE SECTIONS

Section 1

Section 1 is aimed at children of four to five years in Year R. There are 20 units: seven poetry, five fiction, five non-fiction and three drama. The non-fiction units introduce children to different information and ideas based on fact and are restricted to the three genres, report, recount and explanation.

Illustrations provide support to the reading task, which is in caption format. It is important that the units are read through with the children and possible answers to the questions discussed. At subsequent readings it is possible that a number of the children will be able to read the captions for themselves. The number of questions ranges from three to six, to provide progression. They are mainly literal, with some inferential and evaluative questions to prepare children for Section 2.

The reading passages cover topics that should be familiar to the majority of children in this age group. The poetry units include nursery rhymes, with their strong rhythm and characteristic repetition. Rhyme plays an important part in the early stages of learning to read as it gives children the opportunity to extract phonemes, digraphs and letter strings from the words and phrases. This facilitates not only their reading skills but also their spelling skills. The familiarity with the words afforded by the repetition of words and phrases gives children a foretaste of reading fluency and speed which is so essential in later reading tasks.

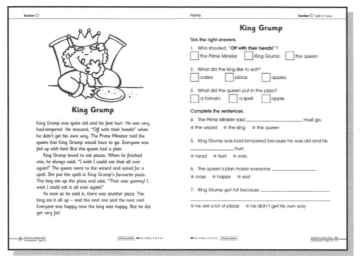

Section 2

Section 2 is aimed at children of five to six years in Year 1. There are 30 units: five poetry, eight fiction, 12 non-fiction and five drama. The non-fiction units cover a wider range of genres than Section 1 and include instructions, reports and explanations; biography, a text type within the recount genre which may be unfamiliar to children of this age group, is introduced.

Progression through each of the genres is provided by the number of comprehension questions, ranging from five in the earlier units to eight in the more challenging units. The comprehension questions are mainly literal and inferential with a small number of deductive and evaluative questions to prepare children for Section 3.

These units provide a more sustained read for the children, and the topics should be familiar to them. As in Section 1, the units should be read through with the children and possible answers to the questions discussed. Children can then go on to complete the units independently.

Section 3

Section 3 is aimed at children of six to seven years in Year 2. There are 35 units: five poetry, six fiction, 18 non-fiction and six drama. The poems and fiction extracts are from published material. The non-fiction units cover a balance of instructions, reports, recounts, explanations and discussions. The units included in the discussion genre, introduced in this section, will give children the opportunity to develop their debating skills as

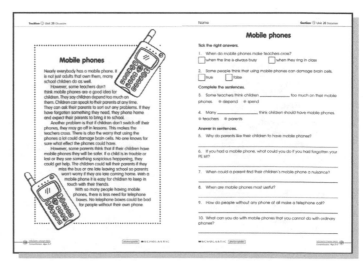

they discuss the pros and cons of the arguments posed. Biographies (recounts) will give them an insight into the impact personalities can have in their time.

The questions increase in number, as in previous sections, with nine or ten in the earlier units and approximately twelve in later units. There is a balance of questions across the full range of comprehension types – literal, inferential, deductive and evaluative.

A greater number of children are deemed to have basic reading and writing skills at this stage, and this expectation is reflected in the responses required to the questions.

HOW TO USE THE ANSWERS

Suggested answers to the comprehension questions for each of the three sections can be found on pages 184–92. At the beginning of each unit, there is a list of how many questions there are in each category – that is, literal, inferential, deductive or evaluative.

In the early stages, particularly in Section 1, the emphasis is on literal comprehension and appropriate answers to the questions could be discussed in small groups. Indeed, there are several units in Section 1 which require oral answers only (see Units 1–3 and 8–9). Discussion should include establishing what form the various answers should take. In Section 1 it is expected that the majority of children will not be able to answer the questions in full written sentences. Instead, they are asked to use tick boxes or provide one-word written answers, as well as carrying out matching and sequencing activities.

Discussion before a unit is completed independently will be particularly helpful to children who need guidance in locating specific relevant information and making appropriate inferences from the text. It will also help them to formulate responses to evaluative questions, when answers depend on their own experiences and preferences. As children gain experience and confidence, they will become more able to work through the units on their own, with the minimum of adult help.

When questions depend almost entirely on the individual's experience and opinions, the phrase 'Own answer' is given. Obviously situations may arise where the children's answers may differ greatly from those suggested. It is usually worth checking the child's understanding and method of expression while also rejecting (though kindly) inventive or purely hopeful answers.

In Section 2, there are more opportunities for written responses, with children being asked to choose from a selection of words and phrases to complete sentences. Then in Section 3, children move on to answering some of the questions in complete written sentences. They should be encouraged to use their own words for their responses rather than repeating sections of the text. It is important that they develop the habit of reorganising and rephrasing the information they take from the text. Their ability to do this will demonstrate their understanding of what they have read.

Poetry genre

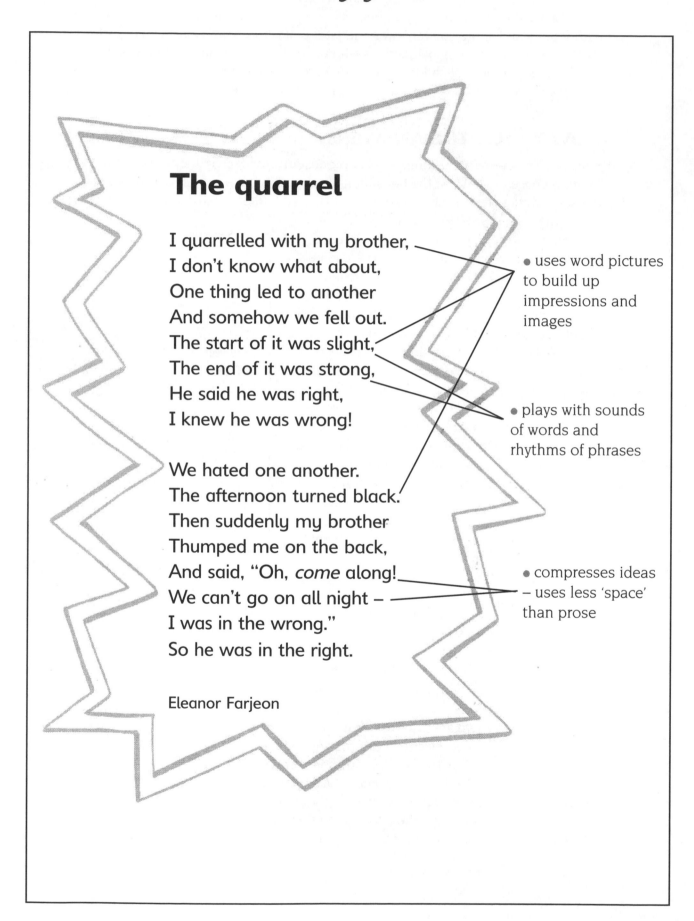

The quarrel

I quarrelled with my brother,
I don't know what about,
One thing led to another
And somehow we fell out.
The start of it was slight,
The end of it was strong,
He said he was right,
I knew he was wrong!

We hated one another.
The afternoon turned black.
Then suddenly my brother
Thumped me on the back,
And said, "Oh, *come* along!
We can't go on all night –
I was in the wrong."
So he was in the right.

Eleanor Farjeon

- uses word pictures to build up impressions and images

- plays with sounds of words and rhythms of phrases

- compresses ideas – uses less 'space' than prose

SCHOLASTIC

Fiction genre

● setting

● involves characters

Why hares have long ears

BEGINNING

Once upon a time a hare made friends with a goat, and they started living together and sharing everything.

One day the goat said to the hare: "Let's build a house!"

"Let's!" answered the hare.

So off they went into the forest for some logs. They came up to a tree and the goat said: "I'll knock this tree down!"

"You'll never!" said the hare.

● dialogue and plot that work together to open the action

"Oh, but I will. I'll just show you!" answered the goat.

And he took a long run, and went Crash! into the tree with his horns, and the tree fell down.

And the hare said to himself: "So that's the way to knock trees down! Now I shall be able to do the same."

MIDDLE

And they came to another tree, and the hare said: "I'll knock this tree down!"

"You'll never!" said the goat.

"Oh, but I will. I'll just show you!" answered the hare.

And he took a long run, and went Crash! into the tree with his forehead!

And the tree still stood where it was before, but the hare's head had gone right into his shoulders.

● presents a problem to solve

The goat saw that he must get the hare's head out from his shoulders, and he caught hold of the hare by the ears and began to pull. He pulled and pulled, till at last the hare cried: "Stop!"

But the goat still went on pulling. He pulled the hare's head back to its proper place, and his ears went way out from his head!

And that's why hares have long ears.

Valery Carrick

END

● ends the narrative with a solution to the problem

Report genre

A fishing competition

- may be in past tense

- focuses on a specific subject area or idea

Angling News

The junior fishing competition was held on Saturday, 8 February. There was a record entry. Eleven boys and seven girls took part. The weather was cloudy with some sunshine. The entrants had come well prepared. They were wearing warm clothes and had picnic lunches with them.

The competition was held on the River Poddle near Radchester. The river fished well and there were some record catches. Josh James tied for first place with his cousin, Susie Sands. The total weight of Josh's catch was 2.56kg and Susie's catch weighed 2.15kg.

Sam Goodman left his rod during the competition to help his brother Jim, who went into the river by mistake. Sam helped him out of the water. Jim was unhurt, but his boots were full of water. The splashing spoiled Sam's fishing chances.

The next competition will be in two weeks. Ring Jack Spratt for details.

- may be a chronological record of an event

- provides facts and examples to support the subject

Recount genre

• usually in the past tense

Mary Anning

• deals in facts

• may involve a narrative structure, for example biography

Mary Anning was born in 1799 in a Dorset seaside town called Lyme Regis. The cliffs by the sea there are full of fossils. Mary's father showed her how to collect them. It was hard and dangerous work. The cliffs could crumble and shower Mary with rocks as she walked along the beach, looking for fossils.

• uses action verbs

Mary was a clever girl. She turned her hobby into a livelihood by selling the fossils she found. When Mary was only 12 years old, she became the first person ever to find a fossil of an ichthyosaur. An ichthyosaur was a reptile that lived in the sea millions of years ago. She arranged to sell her fossil for £23.

• may involve personal observations

• is usually chronological

Mary was also the first person ever to find fossils of a plesiosaurus, another reptile that lived in the sea, a pterodactylus which was a flying reptile, a fish called a squaloraja and a plesiosaurus macrocophalus. All these animals lived 195 million years ago.

• may be a personal account

• contains details

Famous scientists came to Mary's shop to buy her fossils. Her discovery of these "monsters" caused a great stir at the time. When she discovered her plesiosaurus in 1824, she sold it for £100.

Explanation genre

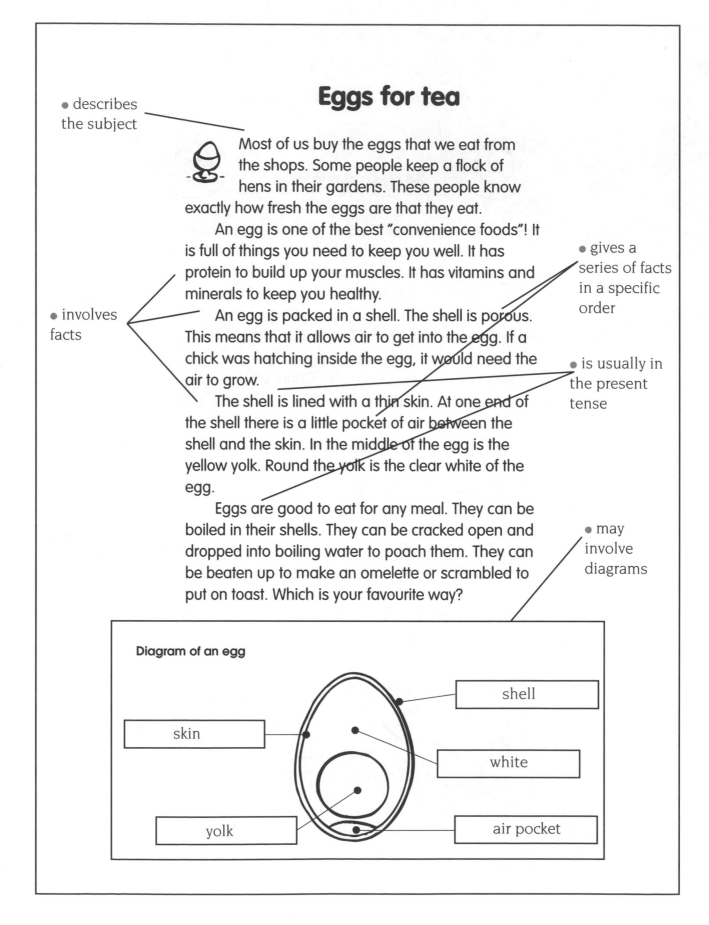

Eggs for tea

- describes the subject

Most of us buy the eggs that we eat from the shops. Some people keep a flock of hens in their gardens. These people know exactly how fresh the eggs are that they eat.

An egg is one of the best "convenience foods"! It is full of things you need to keep you well. It has protein to build up your muscles. It has vitamins and minerals to keep you healthy.

An egg is packed in a shell. The shell is porous. This means that it allows air to get into the egg. If a chick was hatching inside the egg, it would need the air to grow.

The shell is lined with a thin skin. At one end of the shell there is a little pocket of air between the shell and the skin. In the middle of the egg is the yellow yolk. Round the yolk is the clear white of the egg.

Eggs are good to eat for any meal. They can be boiled in their shells. They can be cracked open and dropped into boiling water to poach them. They can be beaten up to make an omelette or scrambled to put on toast. Which is your favourite way?

- involves facts

- gives a series of facts in a specific order

- is usually in the present tense

- may involve diagrams

Diagram of an egg

skin

shell

white

yolk

air pocket

Instructions genre

Coconut meringues

- is usually a series of steps in a specific order (which may be numerical, chronolgical and so on)

Ingredients
2 egg whites
125g desiccated coconut
125g caster sugar
pink food colouring

You will need: a whisk, two bowls, a baking tray, rice paper, a spoon, scales.

- lists materials needed to carry out a procedure

- features action verbs

Method
Whip the egg whites until they are stiff. Fold in the sugar and coconut. Put half the mixture into another bowl and colour it with the food colouring. Pile the mixture in very small heaps on a baking tray covered with rice paper. Bake for 35 minutes at 140°C. Remove the tray from the oven and leave the meringues to cool.

- describes how to carry out a process or procedure

- is in present tense using imperatives

Discussion genre

• has an
opening
statement

• gives area
of concern

Getting to school

Many people worry about the environment. They say we should use our cars less because they pollute the air. We should catch a bus or train instead of using a car. They say we do not have enough exercise so we should walk or cycle to school and work.

However, many parents worry about their children walking to school or using their bicycles. In country areas the roads are narrow and there may not be footpaths. There are very few buses, so people use their cars. This makes the roads dangerous to walk or cycle along.

There are school buses in the country areas. The buses go all round the villages, collecting the children. However, the journey can take as much as an hour for some of the children. But children who do use the school bus can make friends with children from other villages and it is a safe way of getting to school.

In the towns, the roads are very busy. Parents worry that If their children walk to school, it is dangerous for them to cross the roads. Cycling is dangerous too, because of the traffic. There are buses, but the bus stop may not be very near.

Parents want to be sure their children get to school safely. Many parents use their cars because it is quicker and safer. What do you think is the best way?

• a series of reasons or
evidence for the
argument which may
include details and facts

• a closing statement which
sums up the discussion; usually
in present tense

Drama genre

- tells a story via the setting, sound effects and dialogue between characters

Emergency 999

SCENE: *Amir is walking to school with his big sister, Aylesha. They are passing a dark alleyway.*

AMIR: Listen! What's that sound?

AYLESHA: It sounds like someone is ill or hurt. I think it is coming from behind those boxes in the alleyway.

AMIR: Come on! We'd better see!

AYLESHA: There is someone! I can see some legs sticking out from behind that box.

AMIR: Oh! It's poor Mrs Green from our street! What's happened, Mrs Green?

MRS GREEN: Two big lads pushed me over into this passageway. They have taken my purse with all my money in it. I think my leg is broken. It hurts ever such a lot. I can't get up.

AYLESHA: Do you know who these lads were, Mrs Green?

MRS GREEN: Yes, I do! They were those two who live near you.

AMIR: Quick, Aylesha, where is your mobile phone? Do 999 and get an ambulance!

AYLESHA: I'd better get the police too!

(Ten minutes later.)

AMIR: Here they come! I can hear the ambulance and police sirens.

AYLESHA: You'll be alright now, Mrs Green. What a good job I had my phone with me!

- layout and punctuation conventions

- speaker's name; colon

- usually in present tense

- involves what characters actually say

Assessment

Scholastic Literacy Skills: Comprehension Ages 5–7 is valuable in helping you to assess a child's developing progress in English. Comprehension exercises test, above all, children's ability to read and make sense of text. Because the reading passages are appropriately labelled with a particular genre name, it is relatively easy to spot whether a child is less or more able to tackle and make sense of specific types of text. Moreover, by looking at whether particular questions are inferential, deductive, evaluative or literal, it is also easy to recognise areas where the child is having difficulty. In either case, there is a wide range of differentiated material to choose from in the units in this book, which will challenge or build confidence in most children at Key Stage 1.

PHOTOCOPIABLES FOR RECORD KEEPING

Record and evaluation sheet

This has been designed to be completed mainly by the children. It provides a record of the units and allows each child to indicate his or her interest, level of difficulty and level of achievement. It is useful in highlighting individual patterns of needs, interests and strengths. It also builds a strong sense of achievement in each child.

Class record of achievement

This follows the class as it moves through the school, providing a record of what has been covered in each year. It can help teachers find a starting point with a new class, and it can also help with progression between year groups.

Name

Record and evaluation sheet

Fill in the chart for each unit you complete.
Use these symbols or make up your own.

Date	Section/Unit	Did I enjoy it?	Was my work good?	Was it easy?

Teacher's comments

Class record of achievement

Unit	Title	Genre	Date
1	One, two, three, four	Poetry	
2	Ask Mummy, ask Daddy	Poetry	
3	A little frog sat on a log	Poetry	
4	Porridge is bubbling	Poetry	
5	A little seed	Poetry	
6	Little Arabella Miller	Poetry	
7	Two legs sat upon three legs	Poetry	
8	The rescue	Fiction	
9	I like to help	Fiction	
10	The lost shoe	Fiction	
11	The Billy Goats Gruff	Fiction	
12	The elves and the shoemaker	Fiction	
13	Who can?	Report	
14	The story of a butterfly	Report	
15	Where do you live?	Recount	
16	Special clothes	Recount	
17	How do peas grow?	Explanation	
18	Shopping with Mum	Drama	
19	Jam tarts	Drama	
20	Old King Cole	Drama	

Class record of achievement

Unit	Title	Genre	Date
1	Acorn Bill	Poetry	
2	Spider's song	Poetry	
3	If I had a silver coin	Poetry	
4	Hideout	Poetry	
5	When I get up in the morning	Poetry	
6	The lost ring	Fiction	
7	Teddy's new outfit	Fiction	
8	The visit to the dentist	Fiction	
9	The birthday party	Fiction	
10	The very big turnip	Fiction	
11	King Grump	Fiction	
12	The new school	Fiction	
13	The lion and the mouse	Fiction	
14	The classroom	Instructions	
15	Making a leaf print	Instructions	
16	Making a badge	Instructions	
17	Banana and marshmallow cheesecake	Instructions	
18	What melts?	Report	
19	The king of beasts	Report	
20	How many teeth?	Report	
21	Kavita Brahmbhatt	Recount	
22	Keeping warm	Explanation	
23	Acorns	Explanation	
24	Ladybirds	Explanation	
25	Spiders' webs	Explanation	
26	The rainy day	Drama	
27	Oscar's new trainers	Drama	
28	The haircut	Drama	
29	A royal visit	Drama	
30	A mouse in the house	Drama	

Class record of achievement

Unit	Title	Genre	Date
1	A hibernating hedgehog	Poetry	
2	The gerbil	Poetry	
3	The quarrel	Poetry	
4	Monkey tricks	Poetry	
5	Motor cars	Poetry	
6	Finders keepers	Fiction	
7	The beech tree	Fiction	
8	Captain Daylight	Fiction	
9	Geraldine gets lucky	Fiction	
10	Emily and the egg	Fiction	
11	Why hares have long ears	Fiction	
12	Coconut meringues	Instructions	
13	Which way?	Instructions	
14	Going fishing	Instructions	
15	School news	Report	
16	Newspaper story	Report	
17	A fishing competition	Report	
18	Send an e-mail	Report	
19	A missing dog	Recount	
20	Highwayman Dick Turpin	Recount	
21	Mary Anning	Recount	
22	Greyfriar's Bobby	Recount	
23	Eggs for tea	Explanation	
24	Hedgehogs	Explanation	
25	Coconuts	Explanation	
26	Are you what you eat?	Discussion	
27	Getting to school	Discussion	
28	Mobile phones	Discussion	
29	What happened to the dinosaurs?	Discussion	
30	Miss Muffet's new friend	Drama	
31	Emergency 999	Drama	
32	The goose that laid the golden egg	Drama	
33	The coconut shy	Drama	
34	The lost rabbit	Drama	
35	King Midas	Drama	

One, two, three, four

One, two, three, four,

Mary at the cottage door,

Eating cherries off a plate,

Five, six, seven, eight.

Anon

1. What is the little girl's name?

2. How many cherries has she eaten?

3. What type of house does she live in?

Ask Mummy, ask Daddy

When I ask Daddy
Daddy says ask Mummy

When I ask Mummy
Mummy says ask Daddy.

I don't know where to go.

Better ask my teddy
he never says no.

John Agard

1. Who does the little boy ask first?

2. What does Mummy say?

3. Why is Teddy the best to ask?

photocopiable ▰SCHOLASTIC

A little frog sat on a log

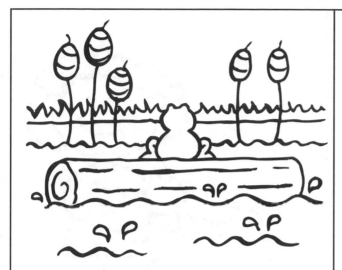

A little frog sat on a log

And said, "Nobody cares about me."

A duck came along
And said, "You are wrong."

And gobbled him up for tea!

Anon

1. What is the frog sitting on?

2. What part of the day is it?

3. Do you think the frog knew the duck was coming?

Porridge is bubbling

Porridge is bubbling,
Bubbling hot,

Stir it round
And round in the pot.

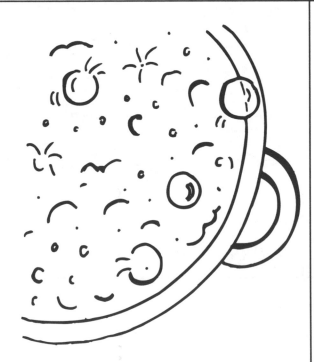

The bubbles plip!
The bubbles plop!

Porridge is bubbling,
Bubbling hot.

Anon

Porridge is bubbling

Tick the right answers.

1. The porridge is cooking in a ....

☐ bowl   ☐ pot

2. While the porridge is cooking, you must ....

☐ stir it with a spoon   ☐ leave it alone

3. When do you usually eat porridge?

☐ for tea   ☐ for breakfast   ☐ for dinner

4. How can you tell the porridge is hot?

☐ It smells good.   ☐ It is bubbling.   ☐ It is ready to eat.

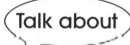

Talk about

What would **you** put on porridge to make it good to eat?

A little seed

A little seed
For me to sow...

A little earth
To make it grow...

A little hole,
A little pat...

A little wish,
And that is that.

A little sun,
A little shower,

A little while,
And then – a flower!

Mabel Watts

A little seed

Tick the right answers.

1. What is the little boy going to do with the seed?

☐ plant it   ☐ keep it

2. He is going to put the seed ....

☐ in his hand   ☐ in the ground

3. What does the seed need to help it grow?

☐ a fork and spade   ☐ sun and rain

4. What will the seed grow into?

☐ a bush   ☐ a flower   ☐ a tree

(Talk about)

What could the little boy do to help the seed grow if there was no rain?

Little Arabella Miller

Little Arabella Miller

Found a woolly caterpillar.

First it crawled upon her mother,

Then it crawled upon her brother;

All said, "Arabella Miller,

Take away that caterpillar."

Ann Elliott

Little Arabella Miller

Tick the right answers.

1. Who found the caterpillar?

☐ Arabella Miller   ☐ Arabella Miller's mother

2. What sort of caterpillar was it?

☐ slimy   ☐ woolly

3. Who did the caterpillar crawl on first?

☐ Arabella   ☐ her mother   ☐ her brother

4. What word in the poem rhymes with **mother**?

☐ bother   ☐ father   ☐ brother

5. What did Arabella's mother and brother think of the caterpillar?

☐ They did not like it crawling on them.

☐ They thought it was funny when it crawled on them.

Talk about

How would you feel if a caterpillar crawled on your tummy?

Two legs sat upon three legs

Two legs sat upon three legs

With one leg in his lap;

In comes four legs

And runs away with one leg;

Up jumps two legs,

Catches up three legs,

Throws it after four legs,

And makes him bring back one leg.

Traditional

Two legs sat upon three legs

Tick the right answers.

1. What is the man sitting on?

☐ a four-legged chair   ☐ a three-legged stool

2. What has the man got on his lap?

☐ meat on a plate   ☐ soup in a bowl

3. What does the dog do?

☐ He eats the meat.

☐ He knocks over the stool.

☐ He steals the meat.

4. The man throws .... at the dog.

☐ the leg of meat   ☐ the stool   ☐ the plate

5. In the end the dog .... the leg of meat.

☐ eats   ☐ hides   ☐ brings back

Talk about

How many legs are there altogether in the poem?

Name

The rescue

1. Why is the boy crying?

2. Why has the little girl gone to fetch her dad?

3. What will her dad do?

Scholastic Literacy Skills
Comprehension Ages 5–7

photocopiable   SCHOLASTIC

I like to help

I like to help wash the dishes.

I like to help make the beds.

I like to help feed the cat.

I like to help make the tea.

1. What does the boy do in the kitchen?

2. Which job does he do in the bedroom?

3. Which job would you like the best?

The lost shoe

I'm looking for my shoe.
Is it in here?

I'm looking for my shoe.
Can it be in here?

I'm looking for my shoe.
Where can it be?

I'm looking for my shoe.
Have you seen it?

I'm looking for my shoe.
Is it in here?

I'm looking for my shoe,
and here it is!

The lost shoe

Tick the right answers.

1. What has the girl lost?

[ ] her dog   [ ] her shoe

2. Where did she look first?

[ ] under the sink   [ ] in her toy box

3. How many places did the girl look in?

[ ] 7   [ ] 5   [ ] 6

4. Where did she find her shoe?

[ ] in the shed   [ ] in the dog's kennel   [ ] in her toy box

Talk about

How do you think the shoe got there?

The Billy Goats Gruff

Three Billy Goats Gruff wanted to cross the bridge to eat the grass in the field.

A big bad troll lived under the bridge. He liked to eat goats.

Little Billy Goat Gruff crossed the bridge. The troll jumped out to eat him up.

"Don't eat me," said the little billy goat. "I am too little. Wait for my brother. He is bigger."

The second billy goat crossed the bridge. The troll jumped out to eat him up.

"Don't eat me," said the second billy goat. "Wait for my brother. He is bigger."

Big Billy Goat Gruff crossed the bridge. The troll jumped out to eat him up.

But Big Billy Goat Gruff hit the troll so hard he was never seen again.

The Billy Goats Gruff

Tick the right answers.

1. How many billy goats are there?

    ☐ 2   ☐ 3   ☐ 4

2. Where does the troll live?

    ☐ in the field   ☐ under the bridge

3. The troll wants to .... the goats.

    ☐ scare   ☐ play with   ☐ eat

4. Why are the goats crossing the bridge?

    ☐ to get to the grassy field   ☐ to annoy the troll

Talk about

What happened to the troll in the end?

The elves and the shoemaker

The shoemaker and his wife worked very hard, making shoes to sell.

They were so tired one night that they left their work before they had finished.

In the morning, they were very surprised to see the work was finished.

That night they were too tired again to finish the shoes.

In the morning, they found six pairs of shoes waiting for them.

The wife wanted to see who was helping them, so she kept watch.

Two elves came in the night and worked away to make more shoes.

The wife was so happy, she made two suits of clothes for the elves to say thank you.

The elves and the shoemaker

Tick the right answers.

1. The shoemaker and his wife were making ....

☐ work   ☐ shoes

2. Why did they leave the work unfinished?

☐ because they were hungry   ☐ because they were tired

3. Why were the shoemaker and his wife surprised?

☐ because the work was finished in the morning

☐ because they could not sleep

4. The wife kept watch one night to see ....

☐ that the work was finished   ☐ who was helping them

☐ if she could stay awake

5. What did the wife do to show she was happy?

☐ She stayed up to keep watch.

☐ She made shoes for the elves.

☐ She made suits of clothes for the elves.

Who can?

A fish can swim.

A mouse can run.

A frog can hop.

A bird can fly.

Tick the right answers.

1. Who can run?

⬜ a fish   ⬜ a frog   ⬜ a mouse   ⬜ a bird

2. Who can swim?

⬜ a fish   ⬜ a frog   ⬜ a mouse   ⬜ a bird

3. Who can fly?

⬜ a fish   ⬜ a frog   ⬜ a mouse   ⬜ a bird

Talk about

What can you do?

Scholastic Literacy Skills
Comprehension Ages 5–7

The story of a butterfly

A butterfly lays its eggs.

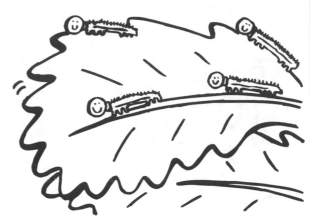

The eggs hatch into caterpillars.

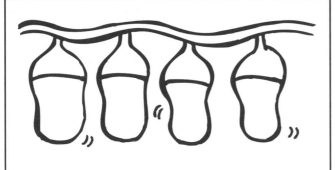

The caterpillars make a cocoon.

The caterpillars change into butterflies.

Tick 'yes' if the sentence is true. Tick 'no' If the sentence is not true.

1. Caterpillars lay eggs.   ☐ Yes   ☐ No

2. Caterpillars change into butterflies.   ☐ Yes   ☐ No

3. Cocoons are made by caterpillars.   ☐ Yes   ☐ No

4. Match the cut-out pictures and sentences to the pictures and sentences on this page.

NOTE TO THE TEACHER: Make a second copy of this page. Separate the pictures and sentences by cutting up the page.

Name

Where do you live?

mouse	bird	snail

I live in a hole.	I live in a nest.	I live in my shell.

me

This is where I live.

1. Draw a picture of your home.

Write in the missing words.

2. A _____ lives in a hole.

3. A _____ lives in a nest.

4. A snail lives in _____.

Special clothes

Cut out these sentences. Match them to the correct picture.

I am a nurse.
I wear these clothes.

I am a policewoman.
I wear these clothes.

I am a firefighter.
I wear these clothes.

I am a postman.
I wear these clothes.

Talk about

Who else do you know that wears special clothes?

Can you draw a picture of this person?

How do peas grow?

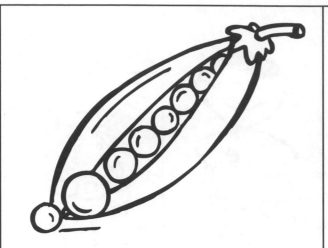

A pea is a seed.

The pea is planted in soil.

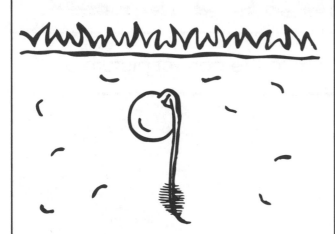

The pea seed grows roots.

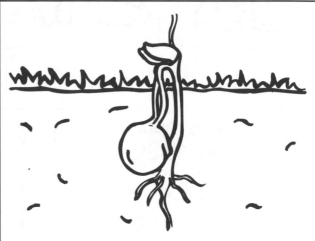

The pea seed grows a shoot.

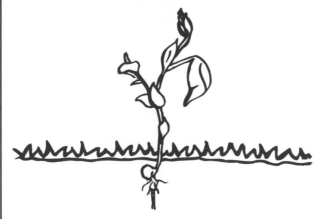

The shoot grows into a
plant with flowers.

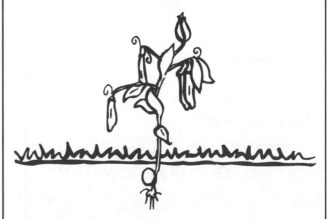

The flowers make pea pods
with peas inside.

How do peas grow?

Tick the right answers.

1. A pea is a ....

☐ root   ☐ seed

2. The .... grows roots.

☐ seed   ☐ flower

3. The shoots grow into a .... with flowers.

☐ soil   ☐ plant

Choose the right word and write it in the space.

4. The _____ make pea pods.

● flowers   ● shoots

5. The pea is planted in _____.

● pods   ● soil

6. Put the pictures in the right order.

NOTE TO THE TEACHER: Make a second copy of the text page. Separate the pictures and sentences by cutting up the page.

Shopping with Mum

TED: Can I get a car, Mum?

MUM: You've got lots of cars at home!

TED: Can I get a pen, Mum?

MUM: You've got lots of pens at home!

TED: Can I get a video, Mum?

MUM: You've got lots of videos at home!

MUM: Oh look! I will get a bag.

TED: You've got lots of bags at home, Mum!

Shopping with Mum

Tick the right answers.

1. .... wanted a new bag.

☐ Mum   ☐ Ted

2. Ted wanted lots of things. He wanted ....

☐ a pen, a video and a hat

☐ a car, a pen and a video

3. Which of these things might Mum let Ted buy?

Put a tick for those he could. Put a cross for those he couldn't.

4. Match the cut-up sentences and pictures.

NOTE TO THE TEACHER: Make a second copy of the text page. Separate the pictures and sentences by cutting up the page.

Jam tarts

QUEEN OF HEARTS: I'll make some jam tarts.
KNAVE OF HEARTS: Can I help?

KNAVE OF HEARTS: They look good!
QUEEN OF HEARTS: They are very hot.

QUEEN OF HEARTS: I will put them on the table to cool.

KNAVE OF HEARTS: I will just have one.
I will take them to my hiding place.

QUEEN OF HEARTS: Where are my tarts?
They have gone!

KNAVE OF HEARTS: Oops! I have eaten them all!
QUEEN OF HEARTS: It was you! No tea for you today!

Jam tarts

1. Draw three things the queen used to make the tarts.

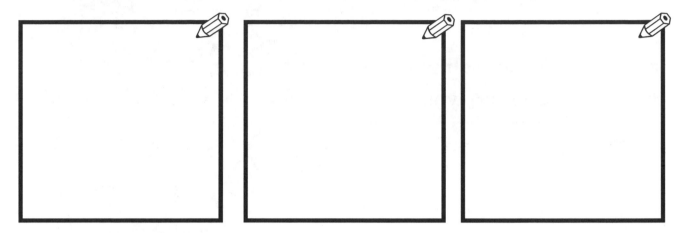

Tick the right answers.

2. Why did the queen put the tarts on the table?

☐ to let them cool   ☐ so that the knave could help himself

3. How may tarts did the knave take?

☐ 5   ☐ 12   ☐ 3   ☐ 8

4. Muddle up the cut-out pictures. Put them back in the correct order.

NOTE TO THE TEACHER: Make a second copy of the text page. Cut out the six pictures.

Old King Cole

KING COLE: Bring me my pipe!

SERVANT: Coming, your royal highness!

KING COLE: Bring me my bowl!

SERVANT: Coming, your royal highness!

KING COLE: Where are my three fiddlers?

FIDDLERS: We are coming, your royal highness.

SERVANT: Shall I light your pipe, Sire?

KING COLE: Yes please, I would like that.

SERVANT: Shall I fill your bowl, Sire?

KING COLE: Yes please, that would be good.

FIDDLERS: Shall we play for you, Sire?

KING COLE: Yes please, that would be fun.
Call everyone for a party!

Old King Cole

1. Match the people to the things they brought King Cole.

2. What else do you think King Cole would like? Draw a picture.

3. What is another name for a violin?

Write it here. _____

Acorn Bill

I made a little acorn man
And inked his smiling face,
I stuck four pins for legs and arms,
Each firmly in its place.

I found a little acorn cup
To put upon his head,
And then I showed him to my friends;
"Meet Acorn Bill," I said.

Ruth Ainsworth

Acorn Bill

1. Write the word in the poem that rhymes with **place**.

_____

Tick the right answers.

2. What did the person in the poem make?

☐ an acorn lady   ☐ an acorn man

3. What did the person in the poem make with the pins?

☐ legs and arms   ☐ hands and feet

Complete the sentences.

4. The person in the poem made a hat with

_____.

● a leaf   ● an acorn cup

5. The person in the poem _____

_____.

● let her friends look at Acorn Bill

● gave Acorn Bill to her friends

Spider's song

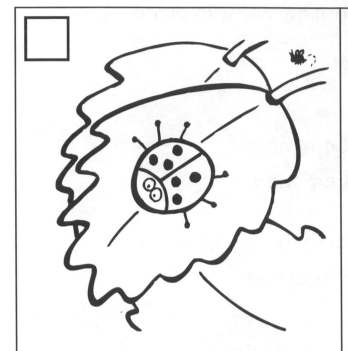

_____ for a ladybird,

Four for a fly,

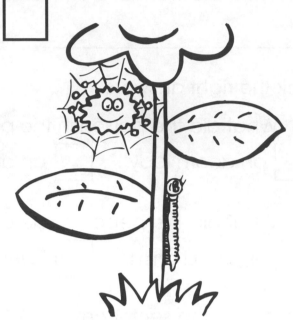

_____ for a centipede

Ready for my tea.

Five for a beetle,

_____ for a bee,

One for a cobweb,

Two _____ for the sky,

Celia Warren

Spider's song

1. On the opposite page, write in the missing number words.

● three   ● six   ● seven

2. Put the pictures in the right order. The first one has been done for you.

Complete the sentences.

3. The _____ is going to have tea.

● centipede   ● spider

4. The names of _____ creatures are in the poem.

● six   ● five

5. The cobweb was made by the _____.

● spider   ● ladybird

If I had a silver coin

And I would buy myself a lovely
Orange lollipop.

I'd put it in the rubbish bin —
I wish I had another.

And when I'd finished licking
I'd only have the stick.

1

If I had a silver coin,
I'd take it to the shop

I'd unwrap all the paper
And I'd lick and lick and lick,

I wouldn't throw it on the
ground,
I wouldn't poke my brother,

Wendy Cope

If I had a silver coin

1. Read the verses of the poem. Put the verses in the right order.
The first one has been done for you.

2. Find the words in the poem that rhyme with

a) lick _____   b) another _____

c) lollipop _____

Tick the right answers.

3. What would the girl in the poem buy if she had a silver coin?

☐ an orange   ☐ a lollipop

4. Where would the girl take her silver coin?

☐ to the shop   ☐ to the rubbish bin

Complete the sentences.

5. The girl's favourite ice lolly tastes of _____.

● lemon   ● orange

6. The girl dropped her lolly stick _____.

● on the ground   ● in the bin

Hideout

They looked for me
and from my nook
inside the oak
I watched them look.

Through little slits
between the leaves
I saw their looking
legs and sleeves.

They would have looked
all over town
except –
I threw some acorns down.

Aileen Fisher

Hideout

1. Write the rhyming words in the poem for

a) nook _____ b) sleeves _____

c) town _____

Tick the right answers.

2. What is hiding the boy?

☐ the leaves   ☐ the acorns

3. How many people are looking for the person in the poem?

☐ one person   ☐ more than one person

Complete the sentences.

4. The person in the poem got the acorns from

_____ .

● his pocket   ● the tree

5. The children were playing _____ .
● hide and seek   ● blind man's buff

6. The boy is hiding in an _____ tree.
● oak   ● apple

7. The boy's friends knew where he was when he

_____ .

● shouted to them   ● threw some acorns down

When I get up in the morning

When I get up in the morning
I tumble out of _____ ,
I yawn and stretch and stretch and yawn
And scratch my sleepy head.

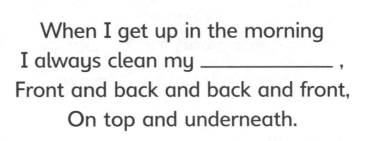

When I get up in the morning
I always wash my _____ ,
And splash and splash the soapy water
All around the place.

When I get up in the morning
I always clean my _____ ,
Front and back and back and front,
On top and underneath.

When I get up in the morning
I always brush my _____ ,
Brush it this way, brush it that,
Brush it everywhere.

When I get up in the morning
I always rub my _____
Because I know my breakfast's waiting –
Yummy, yummy, yummy.

Clive Webster

When I get up in the morning

1. On the opposite page, write in the missing words.

● hair   ● teeth   ● bed   ● tummy   ● face

2. Draw a line to join each picture with the right verse.

Tick the right answers.

3. How does the boy in the poem get out of bed?

☐ He jumps out.   ☐ He tumbles out.

4. What does he splash his face with?

☐ soapy water   ☐ clean water

Complete the sentences.

5. The boy yawns and stretches because he is

_____.

● still sleepy   ● wide awake

6. He cleans his _____ front and back.

● ears   ● teeth

7. The boy is looking forward to _____.

● his breakfast   ● his dinner

8. The bathroom will look _____ when the boy has finished.

● tidy   ● messy

The lost ring

Mum looked sad when she met
Jack from school.

"I have lost my ring," she said. "I have
looked everywhere, but I can't find it."

"Is that the ring Dad gave you?" Jack asked.

"Yes," said Mum. "He'll be worried about it."

"I will help you look for it after tea," said Jack.

Jack had pasta for tea. His mum had made
some little chocolate cakes for Jack. When he was
eating his third cake, his teeth bit on something
hard. He took it out of his mouth. Guess what it
was! It was his mum's ring! What a surprise
they both had!

The lost ring

Tick the right answers.

1. Who had lost a ring?

☐ Jack   ☐ Mum   ☐ Dad

2. Where did Jack find the ring?

☐ in the pasta   ☐ in his pocket   ☐ in a cake

3. How many cakes did Jack eat?

☐ two   ☐ one   ☐ three

4. Why would Dad be worried?

☐ Jack had eaten the cakes.   ☐ The ring was lost.

☐ There was pasta for tea.

5.   Put these sentences in the right order. The first one has been done for you.

◯ Jack bit the ring.

◯ Jack had pasta for tea.

◯ Jack ate a chocolate cake.

① Mum met Jack from school.

Teddy's new outfit

Tina's gran loved to knit. She had knitted Mum a cardigan. She had knitted Ella a scarf. Gran wanted to knit Tina a jumper. Mum said a woolly jumper was too tickly for Tina. Gran looked sad. What could she knit instead? Tina had a good idea. She asked Gran if she would knit a new outfit for her teddy bear. Gran knitted Teddy a jumper, some trousers and a hat. She made them with the wool left over from Ella's scarf. Teddy did look smart!

Teddy's new outfit

1. Match what Gran knitted for everyone.

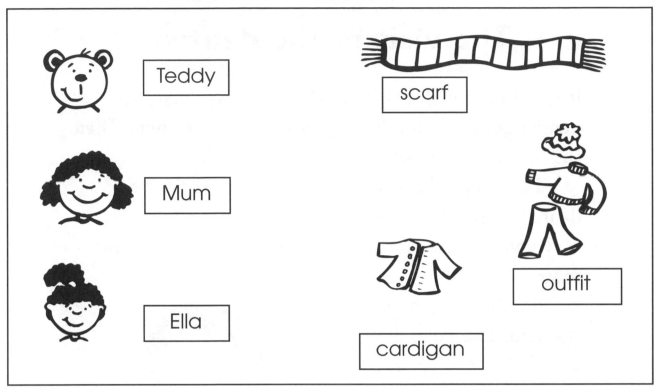

Tick the right answers.

2. Did Gran knit Tina a jumper?

☐ Yes ☐ No

3. What would be too tickly for Tina?

☐ a cardigan ☐ a scarf ☐ a jumper

4. What was the same colour as Ella's scarf?

☐ the teddy bear ☐ the cardigan ☐ the outfit

Complete the sentence.

5. Gran liked to _____.

● read ● knit

The visit to the dentist

It was time for Bobby to visit the dentist. First, the dentist gave him a ride up and down in the chair. Then she looked at his teeth.

"I can see a little hole in your tooth," said the dentist. "I need to mend it for you."

Bobby kept very still while the dentist mended his tooth.

"You have been good," she said. She gave Bobby a smiley badge to wear and a crunchy apple to eat.

"Remember to clean your teeth every night before you go to bed," she said. "It will stop you getting holes in your teeth."

The visit to the dentist

Tick the right answers.

1. Who went to the dentist?

☐ Bobby   ☐ Dad   ☐ Mum

2. What would stop Bobby getting holes in his teeth?

☐ a ride in the chair   ☐ cleaning his teeth

☐ having a badge

3. When should Bobby clean his teeth?

☐ after eating an apple   ☐ when he is at school

☐ when he is getting ready for bed

Complete the sentences.

4. A dentist looks after your _____.

● eyes   ● teeth

5. The dentist thought Bobby had been good because

_____

● he had cleaned his teeth   ● he had kept still

6. Put these sentences in the right order.

◯ Next the dentist mended his tooth.

◯ Then she gave Bobby a badge and an apple.

◯ First the dentist gave Bobby a ride in the chair.

The birthday party

It was Fran's birthday on Saturday. Mum said that their flat was too small for Fran to have a party. This made Fran sad, and she told her friend Jim. Jim's mum asked Fran and her mum to come round for tea on her birthday. Fran's mum said she would make a birthday cake.

When Fran's birthday came, they took the cake round to Jim's house. When they got there, Jim's mum opened the door to let them in. Then the living room door burst open. There was Jim and there were all Fran's friends from school! A surprise party for Fran!

photocopiable **■SCHOLASTIC**

The birthday party

Tick the right answers.

1. Which day was Fran's birthday?

☐ Monday ☐ Sunday ☐ Saturday ☐ Tuesday

2. Where did Fran live?

☐ She lived in a house. ☐ She lived in a flat.

☐ She lived in a caravan.

3. Who took the cake to Jim's house?

☐ Fran and her mum ☐ Jim's mum ☐ Jim

4. Why was Fran sad?

☐ She couldn't have a party at the flat.

☐ She didn't like the birthday cake.

Complete the sentences.

5. Fran and her mum went to _____.

● buy a cake   ● Jim's house

6. Fran's surprise was _____.

● a big party   ● a birthday cake   ● tea with Jim

The very big turnip

Mr Plant put some turnip seeds in his garden. The sun warmed the seeds. The rain watered the seeds. The turnip seeds began to grow. One turnip grew bigger and bigger than all the rest. It grew as big as Mr Plant's garden shed.

Mr Plant tried to pull up the turnip, but it wouldn't come. Mrs Plant helped, but it still wouldn't come. Pat helped, Rob helped, the dog helped and the cat helped, but still the turnip wouldn't come.

Then a little mouse came to help and they all pulled and pulled again. All at once, the turnip popped out and they all fell over! They had turnip for tea for days!

The very big turnip

Tick the right answers.

1. Where did Mr Plant put the seeds?

☐ in the garden   ☐ in the shed   ☐ in a pot

2. What helped the seeds to grow?

☐ the sun and rain   ☐ the dog and cat   ☐ Pat and Rob

3. Why couldn't Mr Plant pull up the turnip?

☐ The soil was hard.   ☐ The turnip was too big.

☐ It was wet.

4. How many helped Mr Plant with the turnip?

☐ five   ☐ six   ☐ three

5. Put these in the order they came to help.

◯ Rob   ◯ the mouse

◯ the dog   ◯ the cat

◯ Pat   ◯ Mrs Plant

Complete the sentences.

6. Mr and Mrs Plant and their helpers _____ the turnip.

● sold   ● lost   ● ate

7. The turnip grew _____ Mr Plant's garden shed.

● by the side of   ● as big as   ● over the top of

King Grump

King Grump was quite old and his feet hurt. He was very bad-tempered. He shouted, "Off with their heads!" when he didn't get his own way. The Prime Minister told the queen that King Grump would have to go. Everyone was fed up with him! But the queen had a plan.

King Grump loved to eat pizzas. When he finished one, he always said, "I wish I could eat that all over again!" The queen went to the wizard and asked for a spell. She put the spell in King Grump's favourite pizza. The king ate up the pizza and said, "That was yummy! I wish I could eat it all over again!"

As soon as he said it, there was another pizza. The king ate it all up – and the next one and the next one! Everyone was happy now the king was happy. But he did get very fat!

King Grump

Tick the right answers.

1. Who shouted, "**Off with their heads!**"?

☐ the Prime Minister ☐ King Grump ☐ the queen

2. What did the king like to eat?

☐ cakes ☐ pizzas ☐ apples

3. What did the queen put in the pizza?

☐ a tomato ☐ a spell ☐ apple

Complete the sentences.

4. The Prime Minister said _____ must go.

● the wizard ● the king ● the queen

5. King Grump was bad-tempered because he was old and his

_____ hurt.

● head ● feet ● ears

6. The queen's plan made everyone _____.

● cross ● happy ● sad

7. King Grump got fat because _____

_____.

● he ate a lot of pizzas ● he didn't get his own way

The new school

Imran's family had moved house. Imran had to go to a new school. He was sad that he wasn't with his friends. All the children in his new class tried to make him happy. By the third day, he began to like school a little bit.

The next day it was raining at playtime. Imran chose a jigsaw puzzle to do. Some of the pieces were missing, so Imran decided to sort out all the puzzles. Everyone was pleased. All the children clapped when Imran was given a badge for helping.

Imran said, "I love my new school and friends."

photocopiable ◼ SCHOLASTIC

The new school

Tick the right answers.

1. Imran had to move house with his ....

☐ friends ☐ family ☐ school

2. Imran was sad because ....

☐ it was raining ☐ he missed his friends

☐ he had lost his cat

3. The children at his new school tried to make Imran ....

☐ sad ☐ happy ☐ forget

4. Imran got a puzzle to do because he ....

☐ was told to ☐ had to play inside ☐ had finished his work

5. Imran sorted out ....

☐ the book corner ☐ the house ☐ the jigsaw puzzles

Complete the sentences.

6. Imran got a _____ for helping.

● star ● badge ● book

7. Imran had been at his new school for _____ days
when he sorted out the puzzles.

● three ● one ● four

8. Number these sentences in the right order.

○ Imran was very happy. ○ Imran missed his friends.

○ Imran moved house. ○ Imran sorted the puzzles.

○ Imran was given a badge.

The lion and the mouse

One day, a lion was asleep in the sun. A mouse ran by. His tail tickled the lion's nose and woke him up.

"Hey!" shouted the lion. He grabbed the mouse in his huge paw.

"Help!" squeaked the mouse. "Please don't harm me. If you let me go, one day I will help you." The lion roared with laughter, but he let the little mouse go.

The next day, the lion was trapped in a hunter's net. He couldn't get free. He roared with anger. The little mouse heard him and ran to help. He nibbled and nibbled at the net until the lion was free.

The lion and the mouse

Tick the right answers.

1. The story is about ....

☐ a mouse and a dog   ☐ a lion and a mouse

☐ a lion and a cat

2. Who was asleep in the sun?

☐ a mouse   ☐ a lion   ☐ a boy

Complete the sentences.

3. The mouse _____ the lion and woke him up.

● pinched   ● tickled   ● bit

4. The lion was going to _____ the mouse.

● play with   ● harm

Tick the right answers.

5. The lion roared with laughter because the mouse

☐ was too small to help a big lion   ☐ had tickled him

6. The mouse nibbled a hole in the net ....

☐ to get in   ☐ to set the lion free   ☐ to get out

7. **Harm** means the same as ....

☐ grab   ☐ hurt   ☐ trap

8. Put these sentences in the right order.

○ The lion was trapped.   ○ The lion caught the mouse.

○ The lion woke up.   ○ The lion was free.

The classroom

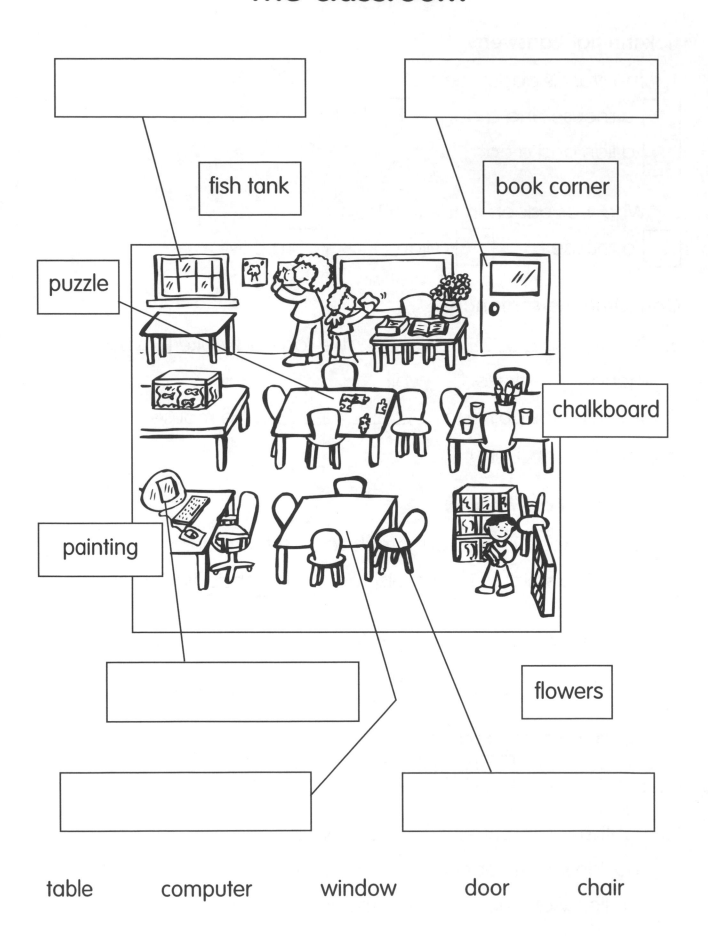

fish tank

book corner

puzzle

chalkboard

painting

flowers

table   computer   window   door   chair

photocopiable ■ SCHOLASTIC

The classroom

Follow the instructions.

1.   Join the labels to the things they match in the picture. One has been done for you.

2.   Write labels for the things in the picture that have been joined to the empty labels. There are some words to help you.

3.   Draw a book on a table and make a label for it.

Complete the sentences.

4.   The boy in the picture is making the book corner _____.

● tidy   ● untidy

5.   The girl in the picture is _____ the chalkboard.

● writing on   ● cleaning

6.   The teacher is putting paintings up on the _____.

● wall   ● window

Making a leaf print

Scholastic Literacy Skills
Comprehension Ages 5–7

photocopiable ◖SCHOLASTIC

Making a leaf print

Complete the sentence.

1. What do the pictures show?

The pictures show how to _____

_____

2. Put the sentences in the right order to make a leaf print. Use the pictures to help you.

◯ Rub over the white paper with some coloured chalk or a wax crayon.

◯ Cover the leaf with a piece of white paper.

◯ Show your leaf print to your friend.

◯ Put a leaf with the flat side down on a sheet of newspaper.

3. Make a list of the things you will need to make a leaf print.

a) _____

b) _____

c) _____

d) _____

Complete the sentences.

4. I could use a _____ to make a leaf print.

● pencil   ● rubber

5. The best time for making leaf prints would be _____.

● winter   ● summer

Making a badge

1. Find something to draw around. This should be the size you want your badge to be.

2. Draw around it on a piece of card.

3. Cut out your shape.

4. Draw and write what you want on your badge.

5. Colour your badge to make it look good.

6. Cut a small square of Velcro.

7. Use some glue to stick the Velcro on the back of your badge.

8. Stick the badge on something you are wearing.

Making a badge

Complete the sentences.

1. The instructions tell you to make a badge from _____.
    ● card   ● paper

2. If my friend was going to be six years old tomorrow, I would put

    _____ on my badge.
    ● Good Luck   ● Happy Birthday

3. The _____ will make the badge stick to your clothes.
    ● glue   ● sticky tape   ● Velcro

4. You stick this on the _____ of your badge.
    ● front   ● back   ● inside

5. If you choose a 2p coin to draw around, your badge will be

    _____. ● a square   ● a circle   ● a star

6. Make a list of all the things you need to make a badge.

    _____

    _____

    _____

Banana and marshmallow cheesecake

Serves 6

Ingredients

For the base

100g crushed digestive biscuits
25g caster sugar
50g melted butter

For the filling

142ml double cream
75g cream cheese
15ml lemon juice
25g caster sugar
3 firm bananas
6–9 marshmallows
chocolate flakes

You will need

mixing bowl
rolling pin
basin
20cm flan dish
wooden spoon
kitchen knife or scissors
chopping board
saucepan
hot water

Making the base

1. Crush the biscuits with a rolling pin.
2. Mix the biscuit crumbs and sugar with the melted butter.
3. Press the crumbs into the flan dish.
4. Put in the fridge for ½–1 hour.

Making the filling

1. Beat the lemon juice into the cream cheese.
2. Slowly beat in the cream.
3. Stir in the sugar, sliced bananas and marshmallows cut into small pieces.
4. Spoon over the biscuit base and sprinkle with chocolate flakes.

Scholastic Literacy Skills
Comprehension Ages 5–7

photocopiable ▪ SCHOLASTIC

Banana and marshmallow cheesecake

Tick the right answers.

1. What is the rolling pin used for?

☐ to crush the biscuits   ☐ to mix the crumbs and sugar

2. What are the crumbs mixed with?

☐ cream cheese   ☐ sugar and melted butter

3. Digestive biscuits are used to make ....

☐ the base   ☐ the filling

Complete the sentences.

4. The top of the cheesecake is sprinkled with

_____.

● bananas   ● chocolate flakes

5. The base is put in the fridge to _____.

● cook it   ● make it firm

6. The sugar will make the cheesecake _____.

● sour   ● sweet   ● spicy

7. The marshmallows can be cut up by using

_____.

● a fork and spoon   ● a knife or scissors

8. This is a good dish for people who _____

_____.

● like bananas   ● do not like cheese   ● like jam

What melts?

An ice lolly will melt, but a lolly stick doesn't.

A jelly will melt, but a bowl doesn't.

A bar of chocolate will melt, but a paper wrapper doesn't.

Butter will melt, but toast doesn't.

What melts?

1.   Make a list of the things in the pictures that do not melt.

a) _____ c) _____

b) _____ d) _____

2.   Put a tick for the things that will melt. Put a cross for the things that won't melt.

☐ an ice-cream cone   ☐ a snowman

☐ a candle   ☐ soap

☐ a candlestick   ☐ a bath sponge

☐ an ice cube   ☐ pebbles

Complete the sentences.

3.   Some things melt when _____.

● they get warm   ● they get cold

4.   An ice cube turns to _____ when it melts.

● water   ● snow

5.   A candle will melt when it _____.

● burns   ● goes out

Put the right word in each space so the sentence makes sense.

6. A _____ will melt,

but a _____ doesn't.

● scarf   ● snowman

The king of beasts

Most lions live in Africa. They like to live where it is hot. Their golden coat matches the sandy desert. This helps them to hide. They sleep in the daytime and hunt at night. The male lion has a big mane round its head and down its back. He has a claw hidden in the tuft of hair at the tip of his tail. Lions have a loud roar. They can make big leaps when they are chasing. Lions belong to the cat family, but they can't climb trees.

The king of beasts

Tick the right answer.

1. What colour is the lion's coat?

☐ It is dark brown.   ☐ It is a yellow colour.

Complete the sentences.

2. The colour of the lion's coat makes it _____.

● hard to see in the desert   ● easy to see in the desert

3. The lion belongs to the _____.

● dog family   ● cat family

4. The lion can't _____.

● climb trees   ● run fast

5. The lion hunts _____.

● when it is light   ● when it is dark

6. The lion likes to live where it is

_____.

● hot and sunny   ● cold and wet

7. What does a male lion have?

Put a tick for all the sentences that are right.

☐ A male lion has spots.   ☐ A male lion has strong legs.

☐ A male lion has a little roar.   ☐ A male lion has a big mane.

☐ A male lion has a tuft at the end of his tail.

How many teeth?

Newborn babies do not usually have any teeth. Their front teeth begin to grow when they are about six months old. Most children have all their "milk" teeth by the time they are two years old. There are 20 teeth altogether.

The front teeth are used to cut food by biting. The back "double" teeth are used to grind up the food. This makes the food easier to swallow.

Foods that are sticky and have a lot of sugar in them will make holes in the teeth if the teeth are not cleaned with a brush.

The "milk" teeth start to fall out when children are six or seven years old. The new teeth that grow in their place have to last for ever!

How many teeth?

Tick the right answers.

1. When does a baby usually get its first tooth?

☐ when it is six years old   ☐ when it is six months old

2. How many teeth could a baby have when it is two years old?

☐ 5 teeth   ☐ 10 teeth   ☐ 20 teeth

Complete the sentences.

3. The _____ teeth are used to bite an apple.
● back   ● front

4. We need our teeth to _____ our food.
● chew   ● suck

5. The **double** teeth make our food _____ to swallow.
● harder   ● easier

6. The _____ teeth grow first.
● front   ● back

7. **Milk** teeth are the _____ set of teeth we have.
● second   ● first

8. If you don't brush your teeth after eating sweets, your teeth

_____ .

● will fall out   ● will not grow   ● will get holes in them

Kavita Brahmbhatt

Kavita's mum and dad are both deaf, so they cannot hear anything. Kavita can hear and she learned to "talk" to her parents by using her hands. There are special signs deaf people can use to talk to each other. When Kavita's baby sister was being born, Kavita helped by "telling" her mum what the doctors and nurses said.

Kavita's baby sister, Payal, is blind. Kavita says she will learn the sign language for the blind. She will learn how to write messages with her fingers on the palms of Payal's hands. Then she can be Payal's eyes as well as being her parents' ears.

In December 2000, Kavita won a national bravery award for being her family's eyes and ears. Her parents, Alka and Rasiklal, are very proud of her.

based on an article in *Woman's Own*

Kavita Brahmbhatt

Tick the right answers.

1. If someone is deaf, it means they ....

☐ cannot see   ☐ cannot hear

2. When Kavita talks to her parents, she uses her ....

☐ voice   ☐ hands

3. How can someone use their hands to talk?

☐ They use special signs.   ☐ They wave their hands about.

Complete the sentences.

4. Kavita helped when her baby sister was born by

_____.

● telling the nurses what to do   ● telling her mother what to do

5. Payal needs Kavita because _____.

● she cannot hear   ● she cannot see

6. In December 2000, Kavita won _____

_____.

● a cup for running   ● a national bravery award

7. Kavita's family need her because _____

_____.

● she works hard at school   ● she can see and hear

Keeping warm

Sheep help to keep us warm. When the winter is over, the sheep's woolly coat is shaved off. The sheep's woolly coat is called a fleece. The fleece is washed to get the dirt and bits out of it. Then it is combed to get rid of the tangles. The next job is to spin the wool. The hairs are twisted together and pulled out into a long, long thread. This long thread of wool is called yarn. It can be used to weave cloth or it can be used to knit things to wear.

Keeping warm

Tick the right answers.

1. **Fleece** means the same as ....

☐ a sheep   ☐ a sheep's woolly coat

2. The sheep's fleece keeps the sheep warm ....

☐ in the winter   ☐ in the summer

3. Which of these things could be made with wool?

4. Number these sentences in the right order.

◯ The fleece is spun into wool.

◯ The fleece is washed and combed.

◯ The fleece is shaved off the sheep.

◯ The wool is used to make things to wear.

Complete the sentence.

5. A sheep would feel cold without its _____.

● fleece   ● woolly tail

Acorns

An acorn is the fruit of an oak tree. The acorn fruit sits in a little green cup. Inside the hard, shiny shell of the fruit is a brown nut. This nut is the seed that will grow into an oak tree. When the acorn is ripe, it falls to the ground. If it isn't eaten by an animal, it will grow into a tree.

photocopiable **SCHOLASTIC**

Acorns

Tick the right answers.

1. What is the fruit of an oak tree?

☐ a leaf   ☐ an acorn

2. What is inside the acorn?

☐ the seed   ☐ the flower

Complete the sentences.

3. Some animals like to _____ acorns.

● eat   ● roll   ● hit

4. When an acorn is ripe, it _____ off the tree.

● flies   ● falls   ● runs

5. The _____ will grow into an oak tree.

● twig   ● leaf   ● acorn

6. Number the pictures in the right order to show how an oak tree grows.

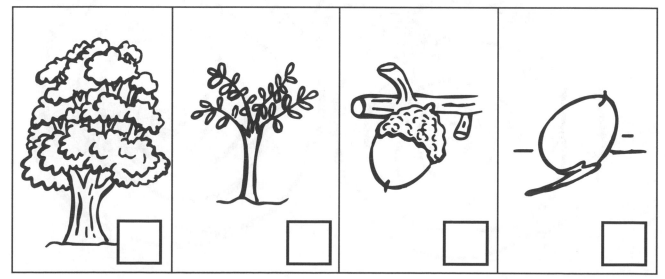

Ladybirds

Ladybirds belong to the beetle family. They are quite small and their back is hard. Some ladybirds are a shiny red with seven black spots. Their wings are under their shiny top. Gardeners like them because they eat the greenfly and other little insects in the garden. These little insects spoil plants like roses and beans.

Scholastic Literacy Skills
Comprehension Ages 5–7

Ladybirds

Tick the right sentences.

1. ☐ Greenfly belong to the beetle family.
   ☐ Ladybirds belong to the beetle family.

2. ☐ Some ladybirds have seven green spots.
   ☐ Some ladybirds have seven black spots.

Complete the sentences.

3. A ladybird can _____.
   ● hop   ● fly

4. Rose plants can be spoilt by _____.
   ● ladybirds   ● greenfly

5. Ladybirds eat _____.
   ● greenfly   ● plants

6. Ladybirds are helpful to _____.
   ● gardeners   ● beetles

Spiders' webs

A spider spins a web to catch its
food. Flies and other insects fly into the
web and get stuck.
A spider makes its web by spinning a
thread. First it makes a square shape. It fastens
each corner to something nearby. Next it spins the
threads across the square so the threads look like the
spokes of a bicycle wheel. Then it spins a sticky
thread to go round and round in circles on the
spokes. The spider makes the centre of the
web very sticky to trap its food. When the
spider has finished, it hides by the
side of the web and waits for its
dinner to come.

photocopiable   **SCHOLASTIC**

Spiders' webs

Tick the right answers.

1. How does a spider catch insects?

☐ It chases them.   ☐ It spins a web.

2. What does the spider do with the insects?

☐ It eats them.   ☐ It lets them go.

Complete the sentences.

3. Insects get stuck on _____.

● the web   ● the spider

4. The stickiest part of the web is _____.

● round the edge   ● in the centre

5. If the spider couldn't catch any insects _____
_____.

● it would get very hungry   ● it would eat the web

6. The insects do not see the spider because _____
_____.

● it has gone away   ● it is hiding

7. Number these sentences in the right order.

◯ Then it spins a sticky thread in circles.

◯ Next it spins threads across the square.

◯ First it makes a square shape.

The rainy day

RAVI: Rain, rain, rain again!

TARA: It would rain on Saturday.

RAVI: Well, we can't go out. Let's tidy our toy boxes.

TARA: Boring!

TARA: I'm going to put all my Lego in this box.

RAVI: I need a box to put my cars in.

TARA: Look what I've found! It's the pen I got for my birthday!

RAVI: And look what I've found! I've found my watch!

photocopiable ■SCHOLASTIC

The rainy day

Tick the right answers.

1. Where are the children?

☐ at school   ☐ at home

2. Why can't the children go outside?

☐ It is raining.   ☐ It is snowing.

Complete the sentences.

3. Tara put her Lego in _____.

● a box   ● a bag

4. Tara thought tidying the toys would be _____.

● fun   ● boring

5. Ravi was pleased he tidied his toys because

_____.

● he found his watch   ● he found his pen

Oscar's new trainers

MUM: It's back to school on Tuesday!

OSCAR: I need some new trainers. My old ones are too small.

MUM: We had better go to the shops.

OSCAR: Can we go on the bus?

OSCAR: Oh! Look at those trainers! Can I have those?

MUM: Let's see if they fit you.

OSCAR: These are great! I'll be able to run fast in these!

MUM: Right, then! Let's see you run all the way home!

Oscar's new trainers

Tick the right answers.

1. Where is Oscar going on Tuesday?

☐ to the shops ☐ to school

2. What is wrong with Oscar's old trainers?

☐ They are too small. ☐ They are worn out.

Complete the sentences.

3. Oscar wanted to _____ to the shops.

● ride his bike ● take the bus

4. Oscar and his mum went to _____.

● a book shop ● a shoe shop

5. The trainers Oscar liked were just the right _____.

● size ● colour

6. Oscar thinks his new trainers will help him

_____.

● get to school ● run fast ● walk home

The haircut

DAD:	Baby Jim's curls look very pretty, but it's time he had a haircut!	
ALICE:	I don't think he's going to like it!	

DAD:	We'll go to the barber next door to the post office. That's where I go.	
ALICE:	I'll bring his tractor to play with.	

DAD:	Come on now! Be a good boy and sit down!	
ALICE:	What a noise he is making! He's gone all stiff!	

BARBER:	I can't cut his hair if he doesn't sit still.	
ALICE:	Come on, Jimmy! Look at me!	

BARBER:	That's better!	
DAD:	Clever girl! You've made Jimmy laugh!	

BARBER:	All finished, thanks to Alice!	
DAD:	Well done, Alice! You can have a special ice cream for being such a help.	

The haircut

Tick the right answers.

1. Who had a haircut?

☐ Dad   ☐ Jimmy   ☐ Alice

2. What was Jimmy's hair like?

☐ It was curly.   ☐ It was straight.

Complete the sentences.

3. The barber's shop was next door to _____.
- ● the post office   ● the garage

4. Alice took _____ for Jimmy to play with.
- ● a car   ● a tractor   ● a ball

5. The barber could only cut Jimmy's hair if Jimmy

_____.

- ● sat still   ● made a fuss

6. Alice made _____ laugh by making faces.
- ● the barber   ● Dad   ● Jimmy

7. Everyone was _____ with Alice.
- ● cross   ● pleased

A royal visit

SCENE: *Lion is talking to Hippo, Porcupine and Grasshopper in a clearing in the wood. Sparrow is perched in a nearby tree.*

LION:	Good news! Owl says Queen Mab is going to visit our wood! What can we do to show her we are pleased to see her?
SPARROW:	Queens love flowers. We could make a garden here in the wood. The queen will have a lovely surprise.
LION:	That is a good idea, Sparrow! But look, the ground is all rough and lumpy.
HIPPO:	I can flatten the ground. I will stamp on it with my big feet. That will make it smooth and fine.
LION:	Well done, Hippo! But we will need to make some little holes in the earth to put the seeds in.
PORCUPINE:	That's easy! I can roll up in a ball and roll over the earth. My prickles will make the holes.
LION:	What a good idea! Then we need to plant the seeds.
GRASSHOPPER:	I can do that! I am light and I can hop from hole to hole to plant the seeds.
LION:	Well done, everyone! Let's get busy!

A few weeks later: Queen Mab is standing by the garden full of flowers. The animals are standing with her. The animals are looking pleased.

QUEEN MAB:	What a lovely garden you have! You must have all worked very hard. The flowers are so pretty. I do love flowers. Come to my palace for a special tea party. Thank you all for a lovely surprise.

A royal visit

Tick the right answers.

1. Who was coming to visit the wood?

☐ Queen Mab   ☐ owl

2. What did the animals plan to do?

☐ have a party   ☐ make a garden

Complete the sentences.

3. Sparrow thought _____ would be a lovely surprise.

● the queen   ● a garden

4. Hippo helped by making the ground _____.

● rough and lumpy   ● smooth and fine

5. Porcupine _____ on the ground to make holes for the seeds.

● ran   ● rolled

6. Grasshopper put _____ in each hole.

● a prickle   ● a seed

7. Queen Mab thought _____ was a lovely surprise.

● the garden   ● the tea party

A mouse in the house

WENDY: Can you look after my mouse for me? We are going on holiday.

LIAM: Yes, I'll put the cage in my room.

LIAM: Where shall I put the cage?

WENDY: Put it up high so the cat can't see it.

GRAN: Look! I've brought you some more shells for your collection.
Shall I put them in your box on the shelf?

LIAM: Yes please, Gran. Thank you very much.

GRAN: Oh help! What was that?
Something jumped out of the box and ran under your bed!

LIAM: Oh no, that was Wendy's mouse!

LIAM: I'll have to go under the bed and look for it.

GRAN: Here you are. Put some cheese in the cage and perhaps it will come for it.

LIAM: That's good, the mouse has gone in the cage for the cheese.

GRAN: We are lucky it was hungry!

A mouse in the house

Tick the right answers.

1. Who looked after Wendy's mouse?

    ☐ Liam   ☐ Gran

2. Liam put the mouse cage ....

    ☐ up high   ☐ on the floor

3. Why didn't Wendy want the cat to see the mouse?

    ☐ The cat might try to get it.   ☐ The cat might be frightened.

Complete the sentences.

4. Liam had a collection of _____.

    ● cards   ● shells   ● stickers

5. The mouse gave Gran _____.

    ● a fright   ● some cheese

6. The mouse ran _____.

    ● out of the room   ● under the bed

7. _____ had a good idea for catching the mouse.

    ● Liam   ● Wendy   ● Gran

8. The mouse went into the cage to _____.

    ● have a sleep   ● eat the cheese

A hibernating hedgehog

A hibernating hedgehog,
Woke up to greet the spring,
He'd set the alarm for half-past May,
But he hadn't heard it ring.
In fact he'd gone and overslept,
silly thing to do.
Not only had he missed the spring,
He'd missed the summer too.

Martin Honeysett

A hibernating hedgehog

Tick the right answers.

1.   The hedgehog had been ....

☐ hopping   ☐ hibernating   ☐ helping

2.   **Hibernating** means ....

☐ sleeping through the winter   ☐ sleeping through the summer

Complete the sentences.

3.   The hedgehog meant to wake up _____ .

● in the summer   ● in the spring

4.   The hedgehog _____

to make sure he woke up.

● slept on a chair   ● set the alarm

5.   The hedgehog did not wake up until _____ .

● the winter   ● the summer   ● autumn

6.   The hedgehog missed _____

by not waking up.

● summer and autumn   ● spring and summer

Answer in sentences.

7.   Why didn't the hedgehog wake up when he should have done?

_____

8.   How long do you think the hedgehog had been asleep?

_____

9.   Who wrote the poem?

_____

The gerbil

The gerbil stands up
Crouching like a kangaroo
Ready to hop;
To him the children he sees
Seem tall as trees;
His paws clutch
The teacher's hand
That stretches like a branch
Above the sand
Of the tiny desert
In his hutch.

Stanley Cook

The gerbil

1. Find the word in the poem that rhymes with

trees _____   sand _____

Tick the right answers.

2. The poem is about .... ☐ a gerbil   ☐ a kangaroo

3. The teacher's hand is being clutched by ....
☐ the children   ☐ the gerbil's paws

4. The name of the .... is Stanley Cook.
☐ gerbil   ☐ teacher   ☐ poet

Complete the sentences.

5. The children look like _____ to the gerbil.
● kangaroos   ● trees

6. The poet says the gerbil looks like a _____ when it is standing up.
● tree   ● kangaroo   ● child

7. The gerbil's hutch is in _____.
● the desert   ● the classroom   ● the bedroom

Answer in sentences.

8. What is on the floor of the gerbil's hutch?

_____

9. What do you think the ground is like where the gerbil lives in the wild?

_____

10. How do you think the gerbil moves about?

_____

_____

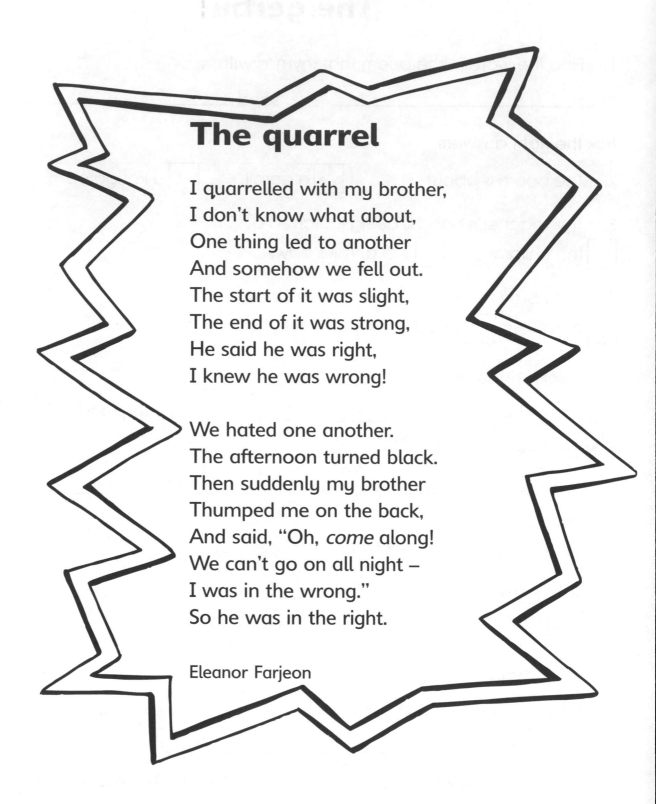

The quarrel

I quarrelled with my brother,
I don't know what about,
One thing led to another
And somehow we fell out.
The start of it was slight,
The end of it was strong,
He said he was right,
I knew he was wrong!

We hated one another.
The afternoon turned black.
Then suddenly my brother
Thumped me on the back,
And said, "Oh, *come* along!
We can't go on all night –
I was in the wrong."
So he was in the right.

Eleanor Farjeon

The quarrel

1. Find two words in the poem that rhyme with **wrong**.

_____   _____

2. Find two words in the poem that rhyme with **right**.

_____   _____

Tick the right answers.

3. There are .... children in the poem.
☐ three   ☐ two

4. The children in the poem had been ....
☐ arguing   ☐ playing

5. What do you think the writer means by saying **The afternoon turned black**?
☐ It started raining.   ☐ The quarrelling got worse.

6. Who is Eleanor Farjeon?
☐ the brother in the poem   ☐ the other child in the poem
☐ the person who wrote the poem

Answer in sentences.

7. Who was the first to try to make up the quarrel?

_____

8. What sort of person do you think the brother is?

_____

9. Who was right in the quarrel?

_____

10. What was the quarrel about?

_____

Monkey tricks

Deep in the jungle
where the sun never shines,
see the Mighty Monkey
swinging on the vines.

Deep in the jungle
climbing up the trees,
see the Mighty Monkey
bend her hairy knees.

Deep in the jungle
where the tall tree grows,
see the Mighty Monkey
scratch her coconut nose.

Deep in the jungle
hear the drums beat,
see the Mighty Monkey
shake her dancing feet.

John Rice

Monkey tricks

1. Find the word in the poem that rhymes with

vines _____   trees _____

Tick the right answers.

2. The monkey in the poem is ....   ☐ in the jungle   ☐ in the zoo

3. The monkey .... on the vines.
    ☐ shakes   ☐ swings   ☐ scratches

4. The monkey shakes her feet because ....
    ☐ the vines are tickling them   ☐ she can hear the drums beat

5. What does the monkey do to climb the trees?
    ☐ swings on the vines   ☐ bends her knees

Answer in sentences.

6. Why does the writer say the sun never shines there?

_____

7. Why do you think the writer says the monkey has a **coconut nose**?

_____

8. How do you know someone else is in the jungle?

_____

9. What do you think would be good about living in the jungle?

_____

10. Write the two lines that are repeated in each verse.

_____

_____

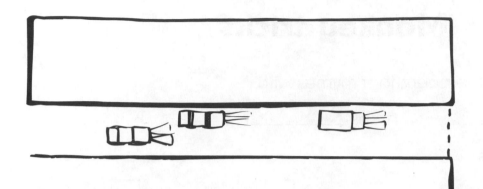

Motor cars

From city window, way up high,
I like to watch the cars go by.
They look like burnished beetles, black,
That leave a little muddy track
Behind them as they slowly crawl.
Sometimes they do not move at all
But huddle close with hum and drone
As though they feared to be alone.
They grope their way through fog and night
With the golden feelers of their light.

Rowena Bastin Bennett

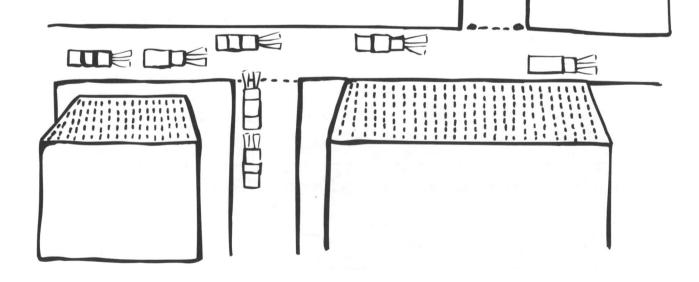

Motor cars

1.   Find the words in the poem that rhyme with:

high _____   black _____   crawl _____

drone _____   night _____

2.   Tick the word that means the same as **burnished**.

☐ shiny   ☐ dull   ☐ speckled

Complete the sentences.

3.   The cars in the poem are _____.   ● golden   ● black

4.   The person in the poem is looking out of the window

_____.

● in the morning   ● in the evening

5.   What kind of home does the person in the poem live in?

_____.   ● a farmhouse   ● a flat   ● a caravan

6.   Where is the person's home?_____.
● in the country   ● in the city

Answer in sentences.

7.   What look like **burnished beetles**?

_____

8.   Why is the window **way up high**?

_____

9.   How fast are the cars moving?

_____

10. What are the **golden feelers**?

_____

Finders keepers

Hannah watched the rabbit hop round the kitchen. Then he settled down to nibble the carrot. She kept very still. When the rabbit moved again, he stopped near her. Hannah stroked him very gently. His fur was dry now. It felt smooth and silky.

"I wish we could keep him," said Hannah. "Finders keepers you know."

"Yes and losers weepers," said Dad. "He must belong to someone. Somewhere, there's a little boy or girl very upset at this moment because he's lost."

Hannah didn't want to think about that.

"We'll just wait for Mum to phone," said Dad, "and then we'll try and find out where he's come from."

Mum was away for the week with the children from her school. If only she were here now, thought Hannah, this might be just the right moment to ask for a pet of my own.

June Crebbin

Finders keepers

Tick the right answers.

1. Does the rabbit belong to Hannah? ☐ yes   ☐ no

2. Where are Hannah and the rabbit?

    ☐ in the garden   ☐ in the kitchen   ☐ in the living room

3. What did Hannah give the rabbit?

    ☐ an apple   ☐ some lettuce   ☐ a carrot

4. What do you think **losers weepers** means?

    ☐ The person who lost the rabbit will be crying.

    ☐ Hannah will lose the rabbit if she cries.

Complete the sentences.

5. Hannah stroked the rabbit and his fur felt very _____.

    ● dirty   ● smooth   ● wet

6. The rabbit's fur had been _____. ● wet   ● dry

Answer in sentences.

7. Why was Hannah's mum not at home?

    _____

8. What will Dad try to do?

    _____

9. Why would it have been a good time to ask for a pet if Mum had been at home?

    _____

10. What will Hannah tell her mum about the rabbit when she phones?

    _____

The beech tree

Rabbit, Goat, Tortoise and Puppy were taking a friendly walk together when they came to a tall beech tree.

Goat stopped and looked up. "What a splendid view of the whole countryside one would get from the top of that tree!" he said. "Upon my word, I could almost wish that I'd been born a squirrel or a monkey!"

"Pooh!" said Rabbit. "It's easy enough to climb to the top of a tree!"

"I bet you ten pence you couldn't do it," said Puppy.

"And so do I!" "And so do I!" said Goat and Tortoise.

"Right," said Rabbit. "All agreed?"

"Yes, yes, all agreed," said Goat and Tortoise and Puppy.

"Right," said Rabbit again. "There's a ladder in Grandmother's garden. If the three of you will be good enough to fetch the ladder, I'll be up at the top of the tree in a twinkling."

"Oh, but Rabbit," laughed Goat, "we didn't agree that you should climb up with the help of a ladder!"

"Nor did we agree that I would do it without the help of a ladder," said Rabbit.

And so the bet was called off.

Ruth Manning-Sanders

photocopiable ■SCHOLASTIC

The beech tree

Tick the right answers.

1. What were Rabbit, Goat, Tortoise and Puppy doing?
☐ playing tag ☐ having a picnic ☐ taking a walk

2. What did they stop to look at?
☐ a beech tree ☐ the lovely view ☐ the wild flowers

3. Why did Goat wish he were a squirrel or a monkey?
☐ so that he could eat nuts ☐ so that he could climb the tree

4. Puppy bet Rabbit that he couldn't ....
☐ climb the tree ☐ find a ladder

5. How much money would Rabbit win from the bet?
☐ 10 pence ☐ 20 pence ☐ 30 pence

6. The words **in a twinkling** mean ....
☐ at night-time ☐ quickly ☐ later on

Answer in sentences.

7. Whose grandmother is mentioned in the story?

_____

8. What was in Grandmother's garden that Rabbit wanted?

_____

9. How did Rabbit plan to climb the tree?

_____

10. Why was the bet called off?

_____

Captain Daylight

Captain Daylight was a highwayman. He wasn't very good at being a highwayman. He didn't even look like a person who robbed people. He was small and round and very cheerful, and he liked telling jokes to the people he tried to rob!

"What goes ha, ha, plop?" Captain Daylight asked his friend Joe, the stagecoach driver.

"Someone laughing his head off," said Joe. He'd heard all the jokes before.

The passengers were sad if their stagecoach *wasn't* stopped by Captain Daylight. They all liked to swap jokes, and stroke Buck, Captain Daylight's horse. They thought it was very exciting to meet a real, live highwayman.

"Did you hear about the man who was so fat that his feet stayed dry when it rained?" said Joe.

They both laughed. They were both *very* fat.

One gloomy Monday morning, Captain Daylight sat at his window. He watched the rain pour down. This isn't very good weather for holding up stagecoaches, he thought. Anyway, why do I do it? Nobody ever gives me any money.

Then he had an idea.

I need to look different, he decided. I shall have to make myself look like a really frightening highwayman. Then everyone will be scared silly when they see me coming.

David Mostyn

Captain Daylight

Tick the right answers.

1. What was Captain Daylight?

☐ a policeman   ☐ a highwayman   ☐ a fireman

2. What did Captain Daylight look like?

☐ tall and thin   ☐ small and round   ☐ old and bent

3. A **highwayman** is a ....

☐ lorry driver   ☐ road mender   ☐ robber

4. A **stagecoach** is a ....

☐ long train   ☐ large lorry   ☐ carriage pulled by a horse

5. Captain Daylight liked to ....

☐ make up lies   ☐ tell jokes   ☐ read stories

6. Joe was Captain Daylight's ....   ☐ father   ☐ friend   ☐ brother

Answer in sentences.

7. Who were the people Captain Daylight tried to rob?

_____

8. Why wasn't Captain Daylight very good at his job?

_____

9. How can you tell Captain Daylight had known Joe a long time?

_____

10. What did he decide to do to make people give him money?

_____

11. How do you think Captain Daylight could make himself look scary?

_____

Geraldine gets lucky

Once upon a time there was a frog, named Geraldine. She lived in a meadow pond with her parents and hundreds of brothers and sisters, uncles, aunts and cousins.

She was lean, green and not at all mean. She was like all the other frogs in the pond, but with one difference.

Geraldine had a dream. She was sure that one fine day she would meet a prince, a handsome prince, with a crown and a castle. He would look at her, he would bend down, pick her up, kiss her and she would turn into a princess. The trumpets would sound, they would be married and live happily ever after.

But when she told the other frogs, they all said, "You don't believe that old fairy story, do you?"

And they laughed so much they fell off their lily pads.

But her mother didn't think it was funny at all.

"What do you want to turn into a princess for?" she asked. "Humans look terrible, a funny colour, small mouths and hair all over the place. Why can't you fall in love with a nice frog with beautiful bulging eyes, a slippery green skin and a gorgeous big mouth, someone who can jump ten times his own length?"

Robert Leeson

Geraldine gets lucky

Tick the right answers.

1. Who was Geraldine? ☐ a little girl ☐ a frog ☐ an aunt

2. Where did Geraldine live?
☐ in a pond   ☐ in a wood   ☐ on a hill

3. Geraldine lived by herself.
☐ true   ☐ false

Complete the sentences.

4. Geraldine was _____. ● a princess ● mean ● thin

5. Geraldine dreamed she would _____ a prince.
● turn into   ● marry   ● fight with

6. Geraldine's dream was like _____.
● a mystery   ● a nightmare   ● a fairy tale

Answer in sentences.

7. How would Geraldine get turned into a princess?

_____

8. Why did everyone laugh at Geraldine?

_____

9. What did Geraldine's mother think?

_____

10. What could a frog do that a prince couldn't?

_____

11. What did Geraldine's mother think of humans?

_____

Emily and the egg

Emily was walking through the park one day when she saw something shining under a bush. She went over to the bush and there, to her surprise, she found an enormous egg. It was bigger than the eggs she ate for breakfast. It was even bigger than her brother's football. It was bright and sparkling and green, and Emily thought it was the prettiest egg she'd ever seen. So she decided to take it home and hide it in the garden shed so that her brother wouldn't find it and take it for himself.

She watched over the egg carefully and went to look at it every day, until one morning, when she opened the door of the shed, she found that the egg had cracked open and the inside of the shell was empty. From the corner of the shed where Daddy kept his lawn-mower came a little curl of smoke. Emily went over to the corner and there, looking at her with round, red eyes, was a little baby dragon. Emily knew it was a dragon because she had seen them in story-books. This one had a green scaly body like a fish, spiky wings and a long, curly tail. When he saw Emily he squeaked and looked frightened, so Emily spoke to him softly:

"Hello, Dragon, I'm Emily. I'll look after you if you like. Are you hungry? I've only got a few chocolate buttons but perhaps you'd like them."

She popped the chocolate buttons into his mouth where they melted straight away on his hot tongue. The little dragon smiled and licked his lips. He put out his claw for more.

Sarah Morcom

Emily and the egg

Tick the right answers.

1. Where did Emily find the egg?

☐ in the garden shed   ☐ in the fridge   ☐ in the park

2. What was unusual about the egg?

☐ It was very smelly.   ☐ It was enormous.   ☐ It was blue.

3. Why did Emily hide the egg away?

☐ Her mother would have been cross.   ☐ She didn't want it to get broken.

☐ She didn't want her brother to get it.

4. Where did Emily hide the egg?

☐ in the garden shed   ☐ in the house   ☐ under a bush

5. One morning Emily discovered the egg had ....

☐ been eaten   ☐ disappeared   ☐ hatched

Answer in sentences.

6. Emily saw a little curl of smoke. Where was it coming from?

_____

7. How did Emily know the creature was a dragon?

_____

8. What did the dragon look like?

_____

Answer in sentences. Use the back of the sheet.

9. How did Emily make friends with the dragon?

10. Why do you think the little dragon's tongue was so hot?

11. What do you think will happen to the dragon in the end?

Why hares have long ears

Once upon a time a hare made friends with a goat, and they started living together and sharing everything.

One day the goat said to the hare: "Let's build a house!"

"Let's!" answered the hare.

So off they went into the forest for some logs. They came up to a tree and the goat said: "I'll knock this tree down!"

"You'll never!" said the hare.

"Oh, but I will. I'll just show you!" answered the goat.

And he took a long run, and went Crash! into the tree with his horns, and the tree fell down.

And the hare said to himself: "So that's the way to knock trees down! Now I shall be able to do the same."

And they came to another tree, and the hare said: "I'll knock this tree down!"

"You'll never!" said the goat.

"Oh, but I will. I'll just show you!" answered the hare.

And he took a long run, and went Crash! into the tree with his forehead!

And the tree still stood where it was before, but the hare's head had gone right into his shoulders.

The goat saw that he must get the hare's head out from his shoulders, and he caught hold of the hare by the ears and began to pull. He pulled and pulled, till at last the hare cried: "Stop!"

But the goat still went on pulling. He pulled the hare's head back to its proper place, and his ears went way out from his head!

And that's why hares have long ears.

Valery Carrick

Why hares have long ears

Tick the right answers.

1. This story explains .... ☐ how to knock down a tree
   ☐ why hares have long ears ☐ how to build a house

2. What were the goat and the hare going to do with the logs?
   ☐ make a bonfire ☐ build a house ☐ put up a fence

3. Where did the hare and the goat find the tree?
   ☐ in the forest ☐ in the park ☐ by the side of the road

4. What did the goat say he could do?
   ☐ climb the tree ☐ cut down the tree ☐ knock down the tree

5. The hare .... the goat.
   ☐ wanted to help ☐ didn't believe ☐ trusted

Answer in sentences.

6. How did the hare think that trees were knocked down?

   _____

7. What happened when the hare crashed into the tree?

   _____

8. What did the goat have to do for the hare?

   _____

9. Why was the goat able to knock the tree down?

   _____

Answer in sentences. Use the back of the sheet.

10. How do you think the hare felt after trying to knock the tree down?
11. How did the hare get his long ears?

Coconut meringues

Ingredients
2 egg whites
125g desiccated coconut
125g caster sugar
pink food colouring

You will need: a whisk, two bowls, a baking tray, rice paper, a spoon, scales.

Method
Whip the egg whites until they are stiff. Fold in the sugar and coconut. Put half the mixture into another bowl and colour it with the food colouring. Pile the mixture in very small heaps on a baking tray covered with rice paper. Bake for 35 minutes at 140°C. Remove the tray from the oven and leave the meringues to cool.

Coconut meringues

1. Number these sentences 1–6 in the correct order.

○ Fold in the sugar and coconut.   ○ Remove the tray from the oven.

○ Put half the mixture into another bowl and colour it with the food colouring.

○ Pile the mixture in very small heaps on a baking tray.

○ Whip the egg whites.   ○ Bake for 35 minutes.

Complete the sentences.

2. The _____ are used to weigh the sugar and coconut.
    ● bowls   ● scales

3. Rice paper is made from _____. ● rice ● paste ● paper

4. Rice paper can be _____. ● washed   ● eaten

5. If you put the cakes in the oven at 10.30am, they would be ready at
    _____. ● 10.35am   ● 11.05am   ● 11.30am

6. **Method** means _____.
    ● what you do   ● what you need

Answer in sentences.

7. Why must you be careful when you take the baking tray out of the oven?

_____

8. How much desiccated coconut would you need to make twice as many cakes?

_____

9. Why do you need two bowls?

_____

10. What would you use to whip the egg whites?

_____

Which way?

◯ Turn left down the road opposite the church towards the village hall.

◯ The surgery is next to the village hall. You will see the sign.

◯ Go about 300 metres along the road until you come to the church, which will be on your right.

(1) First, go down this road until you come to the post office on your left.

◯ Turn right just after the post office.

Which way?

1. The sentences are mixed up. Cut them out, read them carefully, put them in the right order and number them. The first one has been done for you.

Answer in sentences.

2. Which person do you think could live nearby?

_____

3. Which is the first building the man asking the way should look out for?

_____

4. What must the man do when he gets to the post office?

_____

5. Which two buildings does the road opposite the church lead to?

_____

6. Who do you think the man is going to see at the surgery?

_____

7. Who else could the man ask to tell him the way?

_____

8. Make a list of the places the man had to look out for.

_____

_____

9. How will the man know he has got to the surgery?

_____

Answer in sentences. Use the back of the sheet.

10. Write down some instructions which explain how to get from the surgery back to the bus stop.

NOTE TO THE TEACHER: Make a second copy of the text page. Cut out the sentences.

Going fishing

There is a lot to learn about when you first go fishing. Here are some rules to help you get started.

● Wear warm clothes. Two or three layers are a good idea. If you get hot, you can take a layer off. Take a waterproof top layer and wellington boots. Don't wear bright colours as these will frighten the fish.

● Make sure you have a rod licence for your part of the country. Your local tackle shop will tell you which is the one you need.

● Check that you have all the equipment you need such as your rod and reel, a hook disgorger and some bait. If you plan to be there for some time, take something to eat and drink.

● When you get to where you are going to fish, don't make a lot of noise or stamp about on the bank. Fish can feel the vibrations and they will swim away.

● Leave a distance of about 20 metres between you and the other anglers along the bank. They won't be pleased if you are too close to them.

● Don't let your shadow fall on the water and don't make any sudden movements to frighten the fish.

● Make sure you take all your litter home, as well as any bits of fishing line and old hooks.

photocopiable ● SCHOLASTIC

Going fishing

Tick the right answers.

1. Where could you go to buy a rod?

☐ a tackle shop   ☐ a post office   ☐ a supermarket

2. You can be prepared for different temperatures by ....

☐ taking a thermometer   ☐ wearing layers of clothing
☐ carrying a raincoat

3. You must .... before you can fish.

☐ have a plan   ☐ tell other people   ☐ have a rod licence

Answer on the back of the sheet.

4. Make a list of equipment you would need for a short fishing trip.

Answer in sentences.

5. Why isn't it a good idea to wear brightly coloured clothes?

_____

6. Why would other anglers not like you sitting too close to them?

_____

7. Why must you walk quietly and not make a noise when you get to the river bank?

_____

8. Is it better to fish with the sun behind you or in front of you?

_____

9. Why must you take all your litter home?

_____

Answer in sentences. Use the back of the sheet.

10. What do you think you need bait for?
11. List the things that could frighten the fish.

School news

 Dunston Primary School

NEWSLETTER

Welcome back to school after the summer holiday! Welcome, too, to all our new children. I hope they have a happy time at our school.

The playground has been given a new tarmac surface. The markings for hopscotch and the other games have been repainted.

To all parents who bring their children to school by car: could you please park well away from the school gates? This will leave space for the school bus to park near the gates. The children can then leave the bus safely.

Music lessons for the violin and brass instruments will be taking place in school. Tell the school secretary if your child is interested.

Madame Dupuis will come after school on Thursdays as usual. If you would like your child to join the French club, please send a note to school.

The football club will start again next week. It will be after school on Wednesdays. The netball club will be at the same time. The children who would like to join in can give their names to their teacher.

The staff and I look forward to seeing you all at our parents' evening at the end of term.

Mrs Rose Budd

Headteacher

School news

Tick the right answers.

1. When was the newsletter written?

    ☐ at the beginning of the autumn term   ☐ after the Easter holidays

2. What had to be repainted on the new playground surface?

    ☐ markings for parking   ☐ markings for games

3. Who takes a club after school on Thursdays?

    ☐ the school secretary   ☐ a parent   ☐ Madame Dupuis

4. When is the parents' evening?

    ☐ next week   ☐ at the end of term   ☐ after the holidays

5. On which day would you be late home from school if you did netball?

    ☐ Wednesday   ☐ Thursday   ☐ Friday

Answer in sentences.

6. What must parents do if their child wants to join the French club?

_____

7. Which children is the school secretary making a list for?

_____

8. How can you make sure you join the football club?

_____

9. Why can't children be in both the football club and the netball club?

_____

10. What parking problem do you think there is?

_____

Newspaper story

Dunston Primary School

Pupils at Dunston Primary School boost charity funds

Year 2 pupils at Dunston Primary School have been working very hard to raise money for local charities. During the autumn term, the children planted bulbs in flower pots and bowls. The bulbs were ready in time to be sold at the Christmas fair. The sale of the bulbs raised £100. This money was given to the local children's hospice.

Every Tuesday this term, pupils have been making small cakes and biscuits. These are sold at home time. The

Selling cakes and biscuits

money collected will go to Children in Need at the end of term.

Our reporter, Jill Penn, talked to the Year 2 children. She found they had lots of ideas to help people and raise money for charity. Six children will offer to take dogs for walks. Four children

will offer to shop for people who are old or ill. Five children will offer to wash cars. All the class are enjoying collecting toys and games to sell at the school's summer fête. The money raised by these activities will go to local children's charities.

Newspaper story

Complete the sentences.

1. The money the children raise will go to _____.
● school funds   ● local charities

2. The children planted _____ in the autumn term.
● bulbs   ● trees

3. When did the bulbs go on sale? _____
● autumn   ● winter   ● summer

4. **Hospice** means _____.
● a place for travellers to stay   ● a home for sick people

5. The children raised money for Children in Need by _____.
● selling plants   ● selling baked goods   ● holding a Christmas fair

Answer in sentences.

6. Who wrote the report for the newspaper?

_____

7. What did the reporter find out from talking to the Year 2 children?

_____

8. Which two charities are the Year 2 children sending money to?

_____

9. List three ways the Year 2 children have thought of to raise money.

_____

10. Who do you think will be helping the children to organise the things they do to raise money?

_____

11. Think of two more things the school could do to raise money.

_____

A fishing competition

Angling News

The junior fishing competition was held on Saturday, 8 February. There was a record entry. Eleven boys and seven girls took part. The weather was cloudy with some sunshine. The entrants had come well prepared. They were wearing warm clothes and had picnic lunches with them.

The competition was held on the River Poddle near Radchester. The river fished well and there were some record catches. Josh James tied for first place with his cousin, Susie Sands. The total weight of Josh's catch was 2.56kg and Susie's catch weighed 2.15kg.

Sam Goodman left his rod during the competition to help his brother Jim, who went into the river by mistake. Sam helped him out of the water. Jim was unhurt, but his boots were full of water. The splashing spoiled Sam's fishing chances.

The next competition will be in two weeks. Ring Jack Spratt for details.

A fishing competition

Complete the sentences.

1.   The competition was held on _____.
● a canal   ● a river

2.   The weather was _____ on the day of the
competition.
● cloudy but dry   ● wet and windy   ● sunny and warm

3.   _____ is in charge of arranging the fishing
competitions.
● Josh James   ● Sam Goodman   ● Jack Spratt

4.   _____ than ever before entered the
competition.
● Fewer girls   ● Fewer boys   ● More people

5.   The next competition will be held on _____.
● 8 February   ● 22 February   ● 15 February

Answer in sentences.

6.   Why would the junior fishing competition be held on a Saturday?

_____

7.   How can you tell the competition lasted all day?

_____

8.   What do you think the words **The river fished well** mean?

_____

9.   Who won the competition?

_____

10. What happened to Jim?

_____

Send an e-mail

To: stsimons@grasby.cheshire.sch.uk
Subject: A week of weather

Hello everyone in Year 2 at St Simon's!
Thank you for your e-mail giving us your weather report for last week. We hope you had a lot of fun in the snow before it thawed! Our week was cold too, but we didn't have any snow. Here is our weather report.

Monday: Cloudy and overcast. Hail showers in the morning. South-west wind with sunny spells in the afternoon. Maximum temperature 2°C.

Tuesday: Low grey clouds. Rain and sleet all day. Gusty south-west wind. Maximum temperature 3°C.

Wednesday: Grey cloudy sky. Drizzle in the morning. Sunny spells in the afternoon. Light south-west wind. Maximum temperature 5°C.

Thursday: Cloudy sky with blue patches. Sunny spells all day. South-west breeze. Maximum temperature 7°C.

Friday: Clear blue sky. Sunshine all day. Light wind from the south-west. Maximum temperature 9°C.

Let us know how your visit to the glass factory went! Cheers!
From everyone here in Year 2 at Dunston Primary School.

Send an e-mail

Complete the sentences.

1. The e-mail has been sent to _____.
● St Simon's School   ● Dunston Primary School

2. **Thawed** means the same as _____.
● frozen   ● melted   ● cooled

3. The wind was blowing from the _____ all week.
● north-west   ● south-east   ● south-west

4. The windiest day of the week was _____.
● Thursday   ● Tuesday   ● Monday

5. The children of Dunston Primary School could play games outside in the

afternoon _____.
● every day   ● only on Tuesday   ● every day except Tuesday

Answer in sentences.

6. What do you notice about the temperature over the week?

_____

7. Which would be the best day for an outside activity?

_____

8. Which is the worst day of weather?

_____

9. Which mornings had no sunshine?

_____

10. Where had the St Simon's Year 2 children been to?

_____

11. Who sent an e-mail to the children at Dunston Primary School?

_____

A missing dog

LOST!

We have lost our old brown collie dog. She went out last night at 10.30pm. She has not been seen since. She answers to the name of Bracken.

She may not know her way back to us. We are visiting the area on holiday. She could have been trapped in an outside shed or garage. Please could you check?

She is wearing her collar. It has our home address on it. This is 25 Queen's Road, Dunston.

If you have any news of Bracken, please contact Jack and Mary Rose at 31 East Street, Ragford.

A reward is offered.

A missing dog

Tick the right answers.

1. What breed of dog has been lost? ☐ a sheep dog ☐ a collie dog

2. When did the owners last see their dog?
☐ 10.30 at night ☐ 10.30 in the morning

3. Where do the owners live? ☐ Ragford ☐ Dunston

Complete the sentences.

4. The owners are staying at _____.
● 31 East Street, Ragford   ● 25 Queen's Road, Dunston

5. The lost dog's name is _____.
● Jack   ● Dunston   ● Bracken

Answer in sentences.

6. Why might the dog not know the way back to the house?

_____

7. Why are people asked to check their sheds and garages?

_____

8. Why might they try to find the dog?

_____

9. How would they know they had found the right dog?

_____

_____

10. How would people get the dog to come to them?

_____

Highwayman Dick Turpin

Dick Turpin was a famous highwayman in the 18th century. He was born in Essex in 1706. He trained to be a butcher in Whitechapel, but was caught stealing cattle to sell in his shop.

He ran away and joined a gang of thieves and they robbed lonely farmhouses. People were very frightened. News of the robbers was reported in the London Evening Post. Dick and his men were called the Essex Gang. The local constables managed to arrest two of the gang. Dick escaped by jumping out of a window.

Dick became the most famous highwayman in England. He joined up with another famous highwayman, Tom King. They had a hideout in Essex and they robbed anyone who went by.

When Tom got arrested, Dick rushed in to shoot the constables. He was such a bad shot he killed Tom instead. Dick then fled to Yorkshire. He called himself John Palmer and lived like a rich man. One night he shot his landlord's cockerel and was taken to prison. His past crimes were discovered and he was sentenced to death.

On the 19th of April, 1739, Dick Turpin was taken to the gibbet on York racecourse to be hanged. Before the executioner could do his job, Dick threw himself off the gibbet ladder and hanged himself.

Highwayman Dick Turpin

Tick the right answers.

1. Where did Dick Turpin live when he was a boy?
☐ in Whitechapel ☐ in Essex

2. What did Dick train to be when he left school?
☐ a butcher ☐ a robber

3. Dick was .... years old when he was taken to York racecourse.
☐ twenty-five ☐ thirty ☐ thirty-three

Complete the sentences.

4. Dick got meat to sell in his shop by _____

_____.

● robbing farmhouses   ● stealing cattle   ● shooting a cockerel

5. Dick's friend, Tom, was _____ by Dick.
● robbed   ● arrested   ● accidentally shot

Answer in sentences.

6. How did Tom earn his living after he stopped being a butcher?

_____

7. Who did Dick and his gang of thieves rob?

_____

8. Where could you read about the Essex Gang?

_____

9. Who were the Essex Gang?

_____

10. What happened to Dick in the end?

_____

Mary Anning

Mary Anning was born in 1799 in a Dorset seaside town called Lyme Regis. The cliffs by the sea there are full of fossils. Mary's father showed her how to collect them. It was hard and dangerous work. The cliffs could crumble and shower Mary with rocks as she walked along the beach, looking for fossils.

Mary was a clever girl. She turned her hobby into a livelihood by selling the fossils she found. When Mary was only 12 years old, she became the first person ever to find a fossil of an ichthyosaur. An ichthyosaur was a reptile that lived in the sea millions of years ago. She arranged to sell her fossil for £23.

Mary was also the first person ever to find fossils of a plesiosaurus, another reptile that lived in the sea, a pterodactylus which was a flying reptile, a fish called a squaloraja and a plesiosaurus macrocophalus. All these animals lived 195 million years ago.

Famous scientists came to Mary's shop to buy her fossils. Her discovery of these "monsters" caused a great stir at the time. When she discovered her plesiosaurus in 1824, she sold it for £100.

Mary Anning

Tick the right answers.

1. In what year was Mary Anning born?
   ☐ 1979   ☐ 1799   ☐ 1797

2. How old was Mary when she found the first plesiosaurus?
   ☐ 23   ☐ 12   ☐ 25

Complete the sentences.

3. Mary lived _____ called Lyme Regis.
   ● in a county   ● in a seaside town   ● near dinosaurs

4. A _____ is an old bit of a plant or animal that has
   turned to stone.   ● fossil   ● reptile   ● livelihood

5. Walking on the beach could be dangerous for Mary because

   _____ .

   ● she could fall off a cliff   ● she could be swept out to sea
   ● she could be hit by falling rocks from the cliffs

Answer in sentences.

6. How did Mary earn her living?

   _____

7. What was so important about the fossil she found when she was 12 years
   old?

   _____

8. What was a pterodactylus?

   _____

9. Who came to Mary's shop to buy fossils?

   _____

Greyfriar's Bobby

A drinking fountain stands outside Greyfriar's churchyard gates in Edinburgh. On the fountain is a statue of Greyfriar's Bobby with the words, "A tribute to the affectionate fidelity of Greyfriar's Bobby. In 1858, this faithful dog followed the remains of his master to Greyfriar's Churchyard and lingered near the spot until his death in 1872."

Bobby was a Skye terrier. He belonged to John Gray, who was known as Old Jock. Bobby helped Old Jock guard the cattle that were brought into Edinburgh each evening to be sold in the market next morning. Each morning, after work, Old Jock and Bobby went to Mrs Ramsay's café. Old Jock had his breakfast and Mrs Ramsay gave Bobby titbits of food.

Guarding the cattle in the freezing winter winds was very cold. One winter, Old Jock got so cold and ill that he died. When he was buried in Greyfriar's churchyard, Bobby followed his master for the last time.

Bobby stayed as close as he could to Old Jock. He huddled up against Old Jock's gravestone. When he got hungry he went to see Mrs Ramsay and she fed him every day.

Bobby became famous. People came for miles to see him. He was given an engraved collar, a special bowl and official permission to live in the churchyard.

Bobby stayed by his master's grave until he died fourteen years later. Baroness Burdett Coutts had his statue made. Bobby was buried near his master in Greyfriar's churchyard.

photocopiable ◀ SCHOLASTIC

Greyfriar's Bobby

Tick the right answers.

1. Where was the market held?

☐ in the churchyard ☐ in Edinburgh ☐ in the café

2. Who was Bobby? ☐ a cow ☐ a dog ☐ an old man

3. Another word for **fidelity** is ....

☐ faithfulness ☐ terrier ☐ fountain

Complete the sentences.

4. Old Jock was Bobby's _____.
● master   ● mother   ● father

5. Bobby helped Old Jock _____.
● eat his breakfast   ● keep warm   ● guard the cattle

Answer in sentences.

6. Who gave Bobby and Old Jock breakfast every day?

_____

7. What did Bobby do after Old Jock had died?

_____

8. How long did Bobby stay near Old Jock after he had died?

_____

9. How was Mrs Ramsay kind to Bobby after Old Jock had died?

_____

10. Who had a statue of Bobby made?

_____

11. Where does the statue stand?

_____

Eggs for tea

Most of us buy the eggs that we eat from the shops. Some people keep a flock of hens in their gardens. These people know exactly how fresh the eggs are that they eat.

An egg is one of the best "convenience foods"! It is full of things you need to keep you well. It has protein to build up your muscles. It has vitamins and minerals to keep you healthy.

An egg is packed in a shell. The shell is porous. This means that it allows air to get into the egg. If a chick was hatching inside the egg, it would need the air to grow.

The shell is lined with a thin skin. At one end of the shell there is a little pocket of air between the shell and the skin. In the middle of the egg is the yellow yolk. Round the yolk is the clear white of the egg.

Eggs are good to eat for any meal. They can be boiled in their shells. They can be cracked open and dropped into boiling water to poach them. They can be beaten up to make an omelette or scrambled to put on toast. Which is your favourite way?

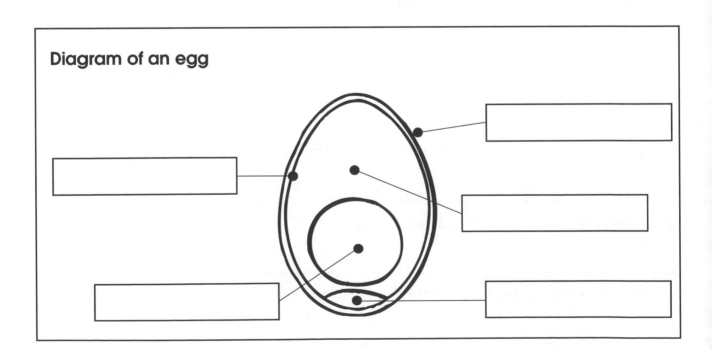

Diagram of an egg

photocopiable SCHOLASTIC

Eggs for tea

Tick the right answers.

1. How does air get inside the egg?

    ☐ through the shell   ☐ through the nest

2. What is good about having your own hens?

    ☐ They are good pets.   ☐ The eggs are fresh.

3. What is the name for a group of hens?

    ☐ pack   ☐ flock   ☐ hatch

4. List three things an egg has to keep you healthy.

    _____   _____   _____

Answer in sentences.

5. Which people would not need to buy eggs from a shop?

    _____

    _____

6. Why does the egg shell need to be porous?

    _____

7. List as many ways as you can to cook an egg.

    _____

8. Say which is your favourite way to have an egg.

    _____

9. What other ways can eggs be used in cooking?

    _____

Answer on the opposite page.

10. Label the parts of the egg.

Hedgehogs

A hedgehog does not look like any other creature we have in the countryside. All the other mammals we may see, such as rabbits, mice or rats, are covered in fur. A hedgehog's back is covered with prickles. Its legs are short and thin. Its tail is short and stumpy. A hedgehog cannot see at all well, but it is very good at sniffing out its food.

A hedgehog sleeps for most of the day under a pile of dry leaves. If you are nearby and very quiet, you may hear it snoring! It wakes up when night comes and hunts for food. Animals that are awake at night are called "nocturnal". When winter comes, a hedgehog makes a comfy bed in a hole and hibernates. This means that it sleeps the winter away.

A hedgehog eats snails, slugs, worms and beetles. It also likes birds' eggs, nuts and berries. It is good at swimming and climbing. A hedgehog has up to seven babies called piglets. They are born in May or June. The piglets are born blind with soft prickles and drooping ears.

Not many animals try to eat a hedgehog. If it is attacked, it can roll itself up into a ball and its prickles keep it safe.

Hedgehogs

Tick the right answers.

1. What makes a hedgehog different from any other mammal we have?
    ☐ It has fur.   ☐ It has prickles.

2. How good is a hedgehog's eyesight?
    ☐ not very good   ☐ very good

3. A **nocturnal** animal ....
    ☐ sleeps all winter   ☐ is awake at night   ☐ sleeps at night

4. Tick three things a hedgehog is good at.
    ☐ hopping   ☐ swimming   ☐ smelling   ☐ seeing   ☐ climbing

5. List four things a hedgehog likes to eat.

    _____   _____   _____   _____

Answer in sentences.

6. How does the hedgehog find its food if it hunts in the dark at night?

    _____

7. What does an animal do when it is hibernating?

    _____

8. Why might some animals sleep all winter?

    _____

9. Why wouldn't other animals try to eat hedgehogs?

    _____

10. What are baby hedgehogs called and when are they born?

    _____

11. What might you hear if you are near a sleeping hedgehog?

    _____

Coconuts

Portugese sailors brought coconuts from India to Europe soon after 1496. It is hard to tell where the coconut palm tree first grew because coconuts float and they floated across the seas.

The tall palm tree can grow up to 33 metres high. In Sanskrit, the ancient language from India, the trees are called "kalpa vriksha" which means "the tree that gives all that is necessary for life".

Portuguese explorers gave coconuts their name because of the three dark spots on the shell. They said the nut looked like a "coco" or "grinning face".

You often see coconuts in shops. On the inside of the brown shell is a firm, white, crunchy layer. The hollow in the middle is filled with liquid called "milk". You can eat the white layer and drink the milk. When the coconut is on the tree, the brown nut grows inside a green case. Inside the case is a layer of coarse fibres. These can be made into mats for the floor.

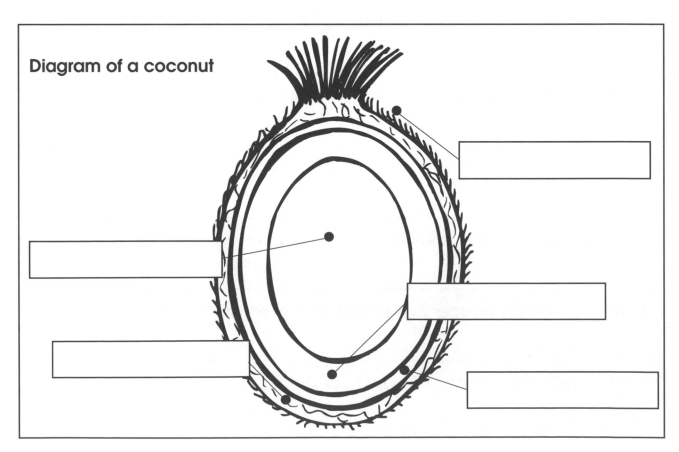

Diagram of a coconut

■ SCHOLASTIC

Coconuts

Tick the right answers.

1. Who brought coconuts to Europe?
☐ Portuguese sailors   ☐ Portuguese soldiers

2. Where were the coconuts found?   ☐ in India   ☐ in Portugal

3. What does the word **coco** mean?
☐ grinning face   ☐ the tree that gives life   ☐ milk

Complete the sentences.

4. Coconuts grow _____.
☐ in the sea   ☐ on palm trees   ☐ on the ground

5. **Sanskrit** is a _____.
☐ type of coconut   ☐ Portuguese explorer   ☐ language

Answer in sentences.

6. Which country does the Sanskrit language come from?

_____

7. What is the Sanskrit name for the plant that coconuts grow on?

_____

8. What colour are the coconuts when they are on the trees?

_____

9. What is coconut matting made from?

_____

10. How would you get the coconut and the milk out of the brown nut?

_____

Answer on the opposite page.

11. Label the parts of the coconut.

Are you what you eat?

Your diet is whatever you eat or drink. Most people agree that a balanced diet is the best. This means you should eat a little of every sort of food.

Some people won't eat any food that comes from animals. They won't eat meat. People who don't eat meat are called vegetarians. Their diet is mostly vegetables, fruit and grains. They say this diet is healthier than a diet that includes meat.

Some vegetarians say it is wrong to kill animals for food. Some people are vegetarians because of their religions and what they believe in.

People who do eat meat say that humans have always been meat-eaters. They say our teeth are the teeth of meat-eating animals and are the right sort of teeth for chewing and grinding up meat. Early man hunted wild animals for food. Wild animals hunted each other *and* Early man for food!

Meat-eaters say that eating meat is a good way of eating the protein needed to build up muscles, bones and other parts of the body. Meat has important vitamins we need to be healthy.

People who do eat some meat as part of their balanced diet can be sure they are eating all the things they need. Vegetarians have to make sure they eat the proteins they are missing in their diet if they do not eat meat.

Are you what you eat?

Complete the sentences.

1. A normal diet is _____.
● what you usually eat   ● eating things you don't like

2. A balanced diet means _____.
● just eating chips   ● eating something of everything

3. Vegetarians are people who _____.
● like meat   ● do not eat meat   ● like to grow vegetables

4. Vegetarians need to make extra sure their diet contains _____.
● protein   ● vitamins   ● muscles

5. Tick the things a vegetarian will eat.
[ ] beefburger   [ ] apple   [ ] rice pudding   [ ] pork sausage   [ ] carrot

Answer in sentences.

6. Give three reasons for being a vegetarian.

_____

7. What do meat-eaters say about their teeth?

_____

8. What does meat have that is good for people?

_____

9. What did some wild animals eat years ago?

_____

10. Why do we need protein in our diet?

_____

Getting to school

Many people worry about the environment. They say we should use our cars less because they pollute the air. We should catch a bus or train instead of using a car. They say we do not have enough exercise so we should walk or cycle to school and work.

However, many parents worry about their children walking to school or using their bicycles. In country areas the roads are narrow and there may not be footpaths. There are very few buses, so people use their cars. This makes the roads dangerous to walk or cycle along.

There are school buses in the country areas. The buses go all round the villages, collecting the children. However, the journey can take as much as an hour for some of the children. But children who do use the school bus can make friends with children from other villages and it is a safe way of getting to school.

In the towns, the roads are very busy. Parents worry that If their children walk to school, it is dangerous for them to cross the roads. Cycling is dangerous too, because of the traffic. There are buses, but the bus stop may not be very near.

Parents want to be sure their children get to school safely. Many parents use their cars because it is quicker and safer. What do you think is the best way?

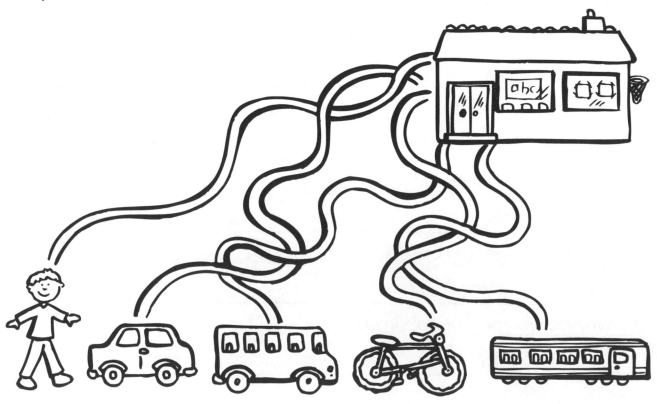

photocopiable ◖SCHOLASTIC

Getting to school

Tick the right answers.

1. What do some people worry about?

☐ the weather ☐ the environment

2. What could people do to get more exercise?

☐ They could walk to work. ☐ They could drive their car.

3. The word **pollute** means .... ☐ to make dirty ☐ to use up

4. Tick two good reasons for using the school bus.

☐ It is safe. ☐ It is fast. ☐ It helps children to make friends.

5. List four ways someone could get to school or work.

_____ _____

_____ _____

Answer in sentences.

6. How do cars pollute the air?

_____

7. Why do parents worry about their children walking or cycling to school?

_____

8. How long might some children spend on the school bus each day?

_____

9. What makes country roads dangerous?

_____

10. Why could walking to school in towns be dangerous?

_____

11. Say how you get to school and why this is best for you.

_____

Mobile phones

Nearly everybody has a mobile phone. It is not just adults that own them, many school children do as well.

However, some teachers don't think mobile phones are a good idea for children. They say children depend too much on them. Children can speak to their parents at any time. They can ask their parents to sort out any problems. If they have forgotten something they need, they phone home and expect their parents to bring it to school.

Another problem is that if children don't switch off their phones, they may go off in lessons. This makes the teachers cross. There is also the worry that using the phones a lot could damage brain cells. No one knows for sure what effect the phones could have.

However, some parents think that if their children have mobile phones they will be safer. If a child is in trouble or lost or they see something suspicious happening, they could get help. The children could tell their parents if they miss the bus or are late leaving school so parents won't worry if they are late coming home. With a mobile phone it is easy for children to keep in touch with their friends.

With so many people having mobile phones, there is less need for telephone boxes. No telephone boxes could be bad for people without their own phone.

Mobile phones

Tick the right answers.

1. When do mobile phones make teachers cross?

☐ when the line is always busy   ☐ when they ring in class

2. Some people think that using mobile phones can damage brain cells.

☐ true   ☐ false

Complete the sentences.

3. Some teachers think children _____ too much on their mobile phones.   ● depend   ● spend

4. Many _____ think children should have mobile phones.
● teachers   ● parents

Answer in sentences.

5. Why do parents like their children to have mobile phones?

_____

6. If you had a mobile phone, what could you do if you had forgotten your PE kit?

_____

7. When could a parent find their children's mobile phone a nuisance?

_____

8. When are mobile phones most useful?

_____

9. How do people without any phone at all make a telephone call?

_____

10. What can you do with mobile phones that you cannot do with ordinary phones?

_____

What happened to the dinosaurs?

There were many kinds of dinosaurs living all over the Earth – on land, in the sea and in the air. They flourished on Earth for 150 million years. Then dinosaurs completely disappeared. No one knows exactly why, but there are several different ideas.

One theory is that the climate became much colder. This stopped the plants growing that some of the dinosaurs ate. When plant-eating dinosaurs died out, the meat-eating dinosaurs had no food, and died too.

Another idea is that a giant rock called an asteroid came from space and hit the Earth. A huge cloud of dust covered the sky. Forest fires started and smoke from them added to the dust. The Earth got cold and dark.

Other scientists say that tiny droplets of water vapour as well as dust were made when the asteroid hit the Earth. When the dust settled, the water vapour trapped the heat of the Sun and the Earth got too hot.

Later, there were volcanoes that erupted. Scientists say these caused dust and gas to block out the sunshine. This made the Earth cold and dark.

However, there are no signs from fossils that there were any sudden changes in the plants or the climate. Perhaps the dinosaurs got a sickness. Whatever happened, it killed all the dinosaurs on Earth. Could it happen again to humans?

photocopiable ▪ SCHOLASTIC

What happened to the dinosaurs?

Complete the sentences.

1. Dinosaurs lived on the Earth for _____ of years.
    ● thousands   ● millions

2. You could find dinosaurs _____.
    ● all over the world   ● in hot countries

3. Another word for **theory** is _____.
    ● weather   ● idea   ● dinosaur

4. Meat-eating dinosaurs ate _____.
    ● men   ● plants   ● other dinosaurs

5. An **asteroid** is a giant _____.
    ● rock from space   ● cloud of dust   ● dinosaur

Answer in sentences.

6. What could happen to plants if the Earth got very cold?

    _____

7. What would have happened if an asteroid had hit the Earth?

    _____

8. What could have made the Earth very hot after the rock hit it?

    _____

9. When volcanoes erupted, what happened?

    _____

10. How do scientists know dinosaurs lived on this Earth?

    _____

11. What do you think happened to the dinosaurs?

    _____

Miss Muffet's new friend

SCENE: *A reporter from "The Nursery News" is talking to Miss Muffet.*

REPORTER: Mrs Hubbard tells me that you had a nasty fright the other day.

MISS MUFFET: Yes, I did! I had just made some cheese and had sat down on my tuffet to eat a bowl of curds and whey.

REPORTER: I like curds and whey too! What happened then?

MISS MUFFET: Well, I was just about to have a spoonful when out of nowhere came this great big hairy spider!

REPORTER: Goodness! What did you do?

MISS MUFFET: Well, I screamed! I upset my curds and whey and my tuffet went flying. It hit the spider on the nose!

REPORTER: What did the spider do?

MISS MUFFET: He burst into tears. He said he never meant to frighten me. He just wanted a taste of my curds and whey.

REPORTER: So did you give him some?

MISS MUFFET: Yes. He gobbled up quite a lot! We are good friends now. He lives in the dairy and catches the flies.

REPORTER: Thank you, Miss Muffet. I'm sure our readers will be glad to hear it.

Miss Muffet's new friend

Tick the right answers.

1. What frightened Miss Muffet?

☐ the reporter   ☐ a spider   ☐ a wasp

2. What had Miss Muffet been doing?

☐ making cheese   ☐ making cakes   ☐ making porridge

Complete the sentences.

3. A tuffet is a sort of _____.
● table   ● stool   ● bed

4. Mrs Hubbard had been talking to _____.
● Miss Muffet   ● a reporter   ● a spider

Answer in sentences.

5. What did Miss Muffet do when she saw the spider?

_____

6. What made the spider burst into tears?

_____

7. What did the spider want?

_____

8. Why did Miss Muffet make friends with the spider?

_____

9. What do you think the spider would like about living in the dairy?

_____

10. What will the spider do with the flies it catches?

_____

Emergency 999

SCENE: *Amir is walking to school with his big sister, Aylesha. They are passing a dark alleyway.*

AMIR: Listen! What's that sound?

AYLESHA: It sounds like someone is ill or hurt. I think it is coming from behind those boxes in the alleyway.

AMIR: Come on! We'd better see!

AYLESHA: There is someone! I can see some legs sticking out from behind that box.

AMIR: Oh! It's poor Mrs Green from our street! What's happened, Mrs Green?

MRS GREEN: Two big lads pushed me over into this passageway. They have taken my purse with all my money in it. I think my leg is broken. It hurts ever such a lot. I can't get up.

AYLESHA: Do you know who these lads were, Mrs Green?

MRS GREEN: Yes, I do! They were those two who live near you.

AMIR: Quick, Aylesha, where is your mobile phone? Do 999 and get an ambulance!

AYLESHA: I'd better get the police too!

(Ten minutes later.)

AMIR: Here they come! I can hear the ambulance and police sirens.

AYLESHA: You'll be alright now, Mrs Green. What a good job I had my phone with me!

Emergency 999

Tick the right answers.

1. How many characters are there in this play?
☐ five   ☐ three   ☐ two

2. Where were Amir and Aylesha going?
☐ to the shops   ☐ to school   ☐ to the park

3. Where was the sound they heard coming from?
☐ from a house   ☐ from a shed   ☐ from the alleyway

4. How did Aylesha know someone was there?
☐ Someone told her.   ☐ She saw a leg.   ☐ Mrs Green waved to her.

Answer in sentences.

5. What happened to Mrs Green?

_____

6. How did Mrs Green know the boys?

_____

7. Why did Aylesha send for an ambulance?

_____

8. What made it easy to get the police and an ambulance to come?

_____

9. What time of the day do you think it was?

_____

10. Do you think Mrs Green will get her purse back? Why?

_____

_____

The goose that laid the golden egg

SCENE: *A cottage in the country. A goose is pecking at the ground. A husband and his wife are sitting outside their door.*

WIFE: I will go and see if there are any eggs. If there are, we could have eggs for our tea.

(Wife goes round the corner of the cottage. She soon comes running back, holding a big golden egg.)

WIFE: Look at this, husband! That goose of ours has laid a golden egg!

HUSBAND: Oh, goodness! We can sell it! We shall be rich!

WIFE: I shall be able to buy a new dress!

(The next day. The husband and his wife are outside their cottage.)

WIFE: Look, husband, another golden egg from the goose!

HUSBAND: You know what this means, dear wife. That goose must be full of gold!

WIFE: Well, we may as well have the gold now. Cut the goose open, husband, so we can get the gold.

(Husband cuts open the goose and peers inside.)

HUSBAND: No gold, wife. Just goose!

WIFE: You daft old man! Why did you say the goose would be full of gold? Now we shall be poor for ever!

Scholastic Literacy Skills
Comprehension Ages 5–7

photocopiable   **SCHOLASTIC**

The goose that laid the golden egg

Tick the right answers.

1. What is the setting of the play?

☐ a cottage in the country   ☐ a caravan park   ☐ a farmyard

2. Which character in the play found the golden egg?

☐ the husband   ☐ the wife   ☐ the goose

Complete the sentences.

3. The husband was pleased about the golden egg because

_____.

● he wanted eggs for tea   ● the egg would make them rich

4. The wife was pleased about the golden egg because

_____.

● she wanted a new dress   ● she wanted eggs for tea

Answer in sentences.

5. How would the wife be able to buy a new dress?

_____

6. How many golden eggs did the goose lay for the husband and wife?

_____

7. What did they expect to find when they cut open the goose?

_____

8. Whose idea was it to cut open the goose?

_____

9. What time of the day did the wife find the first golden egg?

_____

10. How rich do you think the husband and wife are?

_____

The coconut shy

SCENE: *Mum, Dad, Ryan and Jessica are at the carnival fair. They are standing by the coconut shy.*

STALLHOLDER: Roll up! Roll up! Three balls for 50p! Everyone a winner!

DAD: Come on, we'll all have a go! Three balls each, please.

STALLHOLDER: That's right, Sir, all try your luck!

(The family line up in front of the coconut shy and throw their balls.)

RYAN: *(as the stallholder hands Mum a coconut)* Well done, Mum! It was the ball you threw that knocked the coconut off its stand!

JESSICA: *(touching the coconut)* Ooh, it's quite whiskery. And look at these three dark spots at the end of the coconut.

RYAN: *(shaking the coconut)* Listen! I can hear a sloshing sound when I shake it.

DAD: We will make holes through those dark spots when we get home. Then the coconut milk will come out and we can all have a drink.

MUM: And when the milk is drained off, we can saw the shell in half. Then we can cut out the coconut meat and eat it. It's lovely and crunchy! We can hang the shell halves up on the clothes line and let the birds have some coconut too.

RYAN: A coconut is really good. There's something to eat and something to drink. Can we try for another?

The coconut shy

Tick the right answers.

1. The fair has come to the town because ....
    ☐ it is Ryan's birthday   ☐ it is carnival time

2. What is a coconut shy?
    ☐ a stall where you try to knock coconuts off stands for a prize
    ☐ a stall selling coconut shells to be used as bird feeders

3. Who in the family won a coconut?
    ☐ Dad   ☐ Mum   ☐ Ryan   ☐ Jessica

4. What is the liquid inside the coconut called?
    ☐ coconut shy   ☐ coconut meat   ☐ coconut milk

5. Which two words describe a coconut?
    ☐ dry and meaty   ☐ whiskery and spotted   ☐ smooth and hard

Answer in sentences.

6. How much did Dad pay for the family to have a turn at the coconut shy?

_____

7. What could Ryan hear sloshing about when he shook the coconut?

_____

8. How does Dad plan to get the milk out of the nut?

_____

9. What part of the coconut can you eat?

_____

10. How might the children use the two half-shells?

_____

11. Do you think they will try to win another coconut? Why?

_____

The lost rabbit

SCENE: *Ben and his big brother, Will, are in the garden. They are standing in front of a rabbit cage. The cage door is open.*

BEN: *(starting to cry)* Oh no! Snowy isn't in his cage!

WILL: Well, don't start crying, Ben. How do you think Snowy got out? He's clever, but I'm sure he couldn't open the door! You had better try and find him before he gets eaten!

BEN: Oh, don't be so horrid! It must have happened yesterday. I fed Snowy before I went to Beavers, but I was in a hurry. Perhaps I didn't hook the cage door up properly.

WILL: Well, he can't have gone far. Why don't you go next door and ask Mrs Smith if she has seen Snowy? Try Mrs Kang too.

(Ben runs off. Will goes back into the house and switches on the TV. After ten minutes, Ben comes in the back door.)

WILL: Any luck? Have they seen Snowy?

BEN: No. I looked all round their gardens, but I couldn't see him. Poor Snowy, and it rained last night too.

WILL: Why don't you make a notice to put up in the shop? Here's some paper. Make sure you write our address and telephone number. We can take the notice to the shop when we go to school.

(Later that day, Ben is in the kitchen having a drink. Will comes in from school.)

WILL: Hi, Ben! Did you tell your friends about Snowy?

BEN: Yes, but no one has seen him. Listen! There's the phone!

(Ben runs to answer the telephone.)

BEN: Hey! Guess what! It's a girl from the next street! She says Snowy is at her house. Her Dad will bring him back.

WILL: Well, you've been lucky! So has Snowy! You'd better make sure the cage is tight shut in future or he'll be off again!

The lost rabbit

Complete the sentences.

1.   The two main characters in this play are _____.
● friends   ● brothers

2.   The Beavers is the name of _____

_____.

● the people who found Snowy   ● a group Ben belongs to
● the TV programme Will is watching

3.   Mrs Smith _____.
● found Snowy   ● lives next door   ● runs the shop

4.   _____ made a notice to put up in the shop.
● Will   ● Mrs Green   ● Ben

Answer in sentences.

5.   Why do you think Ben called his rabbit Snowy?

_____

6.   How do you think Snowy got out of his cage?

_____

7.   Why was Ben worried that Snowy had been out all night?

_____

8.   What does Ben do to try to find Snowy?

_____

9.   Who found Snowy?

_____

10.   What did Will say to frighten Ben when Snowy went missing?

_____

King Midas

SCENE: *Ancient Greece. King Midas, who loves gold more than anything else, is talking to the god, Dionysus. Dionysus has been staying with King Midas.*

KING MIDAS: *(to Dionysus)* Your stay with me is almost over, my friend. Before you go I must show you my pride and joy – my gold!

(He opens his treasury door to reveal his great store of gold.)

DIONYSUS: My goodness! Your treasury is almost overflowing with gold!

KING MIDAS: Yes, but I still want more and more. I want more gold than anyone in the world.

DIONYSUS: Don't you think that's just a bit greedy?

KING MIDAS: Of course not! I'm not greedy. I'm just very fond of gold.

(He and Dionysus walk out of the palace.)

DIONYSUS: You have made me very welcome in your home, Midas. I would like to leave you with a gift of thanks from the gods. What would you like?

KING MIDAS: That's easy – gold!

DIONYSUS: *(looking at King Midas thoughtfully)* Of course, but are you sure that you want more gold? There are other things in life, you know.

KING MIDAS: Not for me. *(He rubs his hands together.)* Gold, beautiful gold! I love it!

DIONYSUS: *(after thinking for a bit)* All right then, here is your gift. From now on, everything you touch will turn to gold.

MIDAS: *(amazed)* Everything? You mean…? That's wonderful! What a splendid gift!

(He moves to shake hands with Dionysus, but Dionysus quickly moves out of the way.)

DIONYSUS: *(leaving)* Farewell, Midas, and be careful. Remember, everything you touch will turn to gold.

King Midas

Tick the right answers.

1. The two characters in this play are ....

☐ a king and a queen   ☐ a king and a Greek god

2. King Midas asks Dionysus for ....

☐ more gold   ☐ more gifts   ☐ more land

3. A **treasury** is a ....

☐ money purse   ☐ storage room for money   ☐ jewelled crown

4. What does King Midas mean when he says his gold is his **pride and joy**?

☐ His gold is his favourite thing.   ☐ His gold is locked away safely.

Complete the sentences.

5. King Midas was a very _____ man.

● kind   ● unhappy   ● greedy

6. Dionysus could give King Midas anything he wanted because

_____.

● Dionysus was a rich man   ● Dionysus was a god

7. Dionysus said, **"Everything you touch will turn to gold."** He wanted

_____.

● to teach King Midas a lesson   ● to make King Midas happy

Answer in sentences. Use the back of the sheet.

8. Why did Dionysus want to give King Midas a gift?

9. What gift did Dionysus give King Midas?

10. Why did Dionysus move out of the way when King Midas tried to shake hands with him?

11. Do you think the gift Dionysus gave King Midas will make him happy? Why?

12. What do you think will happen to King Midas?

Answers

Section 1

Unit 1: One, two, three, four
Question types: 2 literal, 1 inferential
1. The little girl's name is Mary.
2. She has eaten four cherries.
3. She lives in a cottage.

Unit 2: Ask Mummy, ask Daddy
Question types: 3 literal
1. The little boy asks Daddy first.
2. Mummy says, 'Ask Daddy.'
3. Teddy never says no.

Unit 3: A little frog sat on a log
Question types: 1 literal, 1 inferential, 1 evaluative
1. The frog is sitting on a log.
2. It is the afternoon.
3. Own answer.

Unit 4: Porridge is bubbling
Question types: 1 literal, 2 inferential, 1 deductive, 1 evaluative
1. pot.
2. stir it with a spoon.
3. for breakfast.
4. It is bubbling.
Talk about: own answer.

Unit 5: A little seed
Question types: 2 literal, 2 inferential, 1 deductive
1. plant it.
2. in the ground.
3. sun and rain.
4. a flower.
Talk about: the little boy could water it.

Unit 6: Little Arabella Miller
Question types: 4 literal, 1 inferential, 1 evaluative
1. Arabella Miller.
2. woolly.
3. her mother.
4. brother.
5. They did not like it crawling on them.
Talk about: own answer.

Unit 7: Two legs sat upon three legs
Question types: 3 literal, 3 inferential
1. a three-legged stool.
2. meat on a plate.
3. He steals the meat.
4. the stool.
5. brings back.
Talk about: there are ten legs in the poem.

Unit 8: The rescue
Question types: 2 inferential, 1 evaluative
1. The boy is crying because the kitten is stuck in the tree.
2. She is going to ask her dad to help the boy.
3. Own answer.

Unit 9: I like to help
Question types: 2 literal, 1 evaluative
1. The boy helps to wash the dishes, feed the cat and make the tea.
2. He helps to make the beds.
3. Own answer.

Unit 10: The lost shoe
Question types: 3 literal, 1 inferential, 1 evaluative
1. her shoe.
2. under the sink.
3. 6.
4. in the dog's kennel.
Talk about: own answer.

Unit 11: The Billy Goats Gruff
Question types: 4 literal, 1 evaluative
1. 3.
2. under the bridge.
3. eat.
4. to get to the grassy field.
Talk about: own answer.

Unit 12: The elves and the shoemaker
Question types: 5 literal
1. shoes.
2. because they were tired.
3. because the work was finished in the morning.
4. who was helping them.
5. She made suits of clothes for the elves.

Unit 13: Who can?
Question types: 3 literal, 1 evaluative
1. a mouse.
2. a fish.
3. a bird.
Talk about: own answer.

Unit 14: The story of a butterfly
Question types: 2 literal, 2 inferential
1. No.
2. Yes.
3. Yes.
4. Sentence 1 to picture 1, and so on.

Unit 15: Where do you live?
Question types: 1 evaluative, 3 literal
1. Own answer.
2. mouse.
3. bird.
4. a shell.

Section ① *cont.*

Unit 16: Special clothes
Question types: 4 inferential, 1 evaluative
First sentence matches third picture.
Second sentence matches first picture.
Third sentence matches fourth picture.
Fourth sentence matches second picture.
Talk about: own answer.

Unit 17: How do peas grow?
Question types: 5 literal, 1 inferential
1. seed.
2. seed.
3. plant.
4. flowers.
5. soil.
6. Pictures should be sequenced in the order given in the text.

Unit 18: Shopping with Mum
Question types: 2 literal, 1 evaluative, 1 inferential
1. Mum.
2. a car, a pen and a video.
3. Tick: ice cream, apple, book
   Cross: saw, knife, alligator
4. Text 1 to picture 1, and so on.

Unit 19: Jam tarts
Question types: 1 literal, 3 inferential
1. Drawings should include a jar of jam, a rolling pin and a bowl with pastry in it.
2. to let them cool.
3. 12.
4. Pictures should be arranged in the correct sequence of events.

Unit 20: Old King Cole
Question types: 1 literal, 1 inferential, 1 evaluative
1. Picture of manservant matches pipe
   maid matches bowl
   fiddler matches violin.
2. Own answer.
3. fiddle.

Section ②

Unit 1: Acorn Bill
Question types: 3 literal, 2 inferential
1. face.
2. an acorn man.
3. legs and arms.
4. an acorn cup.
5. let her friends look at Acorn Bill.

Unit 2: Spider's song
Question types: 1 literal, 4 inferential
1. Three for a ladybird
   Seven for a centipede
   Six for a bee.
2. The pictures should be sequenced numerically according to the poem – 2, 4, 3, 1 (from left to right). The poem then reads:
   One for a cobweb,
   Two for the sky,
   Three for a ladybird,
   Four for a fly,
   Five for a beetle,
   Six for a bee,
   Seven for a centipede
   Ready for my tea.
3. spider.
4. five.
5. spider.

Unit 3: If I had a silver coin
Question types: 3 literal, 3 inferential
1. The verses should be numbered 2, 6, 4, 1, 3, 5 (from left to right). The poem then reads:
   If I had a silver coin,
   I'd take it to the shop
   And I would buy myself a lovely
   Orange lollipop.
   I'd unwrap all the paper
   And I'd lick and lick and lick,
   And when I'd finished licking
   I'd only have the stick.
   I wouldn't throw it on the ground,
   I wouldn't poke my brother,
   I'd put it in the rubbish bin —
   I wish I had another.
2. a) stick   b) brother   c) shop.
3. a lollipop.
4. to the shop.
5. orange.
6. in the bin.

Unit 4: Hideout
Question types: 3 literal, 3 inferential, 1 deductive
1. a) look b) leaves c) down.
2. the leaves.
3. more than one person.
4. the tree.
5. hide and seek.
6. oak.
7. threw some acorns down.

Unit 5: When I get up in the morning
Question types: 4 literal, 3 inferential, 1 deductive
1. bed, face, teeth, hair, tummy.
2. Verse 1 matches the boy yawning (bottom left)
   Verse 2 matches the boy washing his face (bottom illustration)
   Verse 3 matches the boy cleaning his teeth (top left)
   Verse 4 matches the boy brushing his hair (bottom right)
   Verse 5 matches the boy rubbing his tummy (top right).
3. He tumbles out.
4. soapy water.
5. still sleepy.

Section 2 cont.

6. teeth.
7. his breakfast.
8. messy.

Unit 6: The lost ring
Question types: 3 literal, 2 inferential
1. Mum.
2. in a cake.
3. three.
4. The ring was lost.
5. The correct order is 4, 2, 3, 1. The sentences then read:
   Mum met Jack from school.
   Jack had pasta for tea.
   Jack ate a chocolate cake.
   Jack bit the ring.

Unit 7: Teddy's new outfit
Question types: 3 literal, 2 inferential
1. The matching pairs are:
   Teddy and outfit
   Ella and scarf
   Mum and cardigan.
2. No.
3. a jumper.
4. the outfit.
5. knit.

Unit 8: The visit to the dentist
Question types: 3 literal, 3 inferential
1. Bobby.
2. cleaning his teeth.
3. when he is getting ready for bed.
4. teeth.
5. he had kept still.
6. The correct order is 2, 3, 1. The sentences then read:
   First the dentist gave Bobby a ride in the chair.
   Next the dentist mended his tooth.
   Then she gave Bobby a badge and an apple.

Unit 9: The birthday party
Question types: 5 literal, 1 inferential
1. Saturday.
2. She lived in a flat.
3. Fran and her mum.
4. She couldn't have a party at the flat.
5. Jim's house.
6. a big party.

Unit 10: The very big turnip
Question types: 3 literal, 4 inferential
1. in the garden.
2. the sun and rain.
3. The turnip was too big.
4. six.
5. 3, 4, 2, 6, 5, 1: Mrs Plant, Pat, Rob, the dog, the cat, the mouse
6. ate.
7. as big as.

Unit 11: King Grump
Question types: 4 literal, 3 inferential
1. King Grump.
2. pizzas.
3. a spell.
4. the king.
5. feet.
6. happy.
7. he ate a lot of pizzas.

Unit 12: The new school
Question types: 5 literal, 3 inferential
1. family.
2. he missed his friends.
3. happy.
4. had to play inside.
5. the jigsaw puzzles.
6. badge.
7. four.
8. 5, 1, 4, 2, 3:
   Imran moved house.
   Imran missed his friends.
   Imran sorted the puzzles.
   Imran was given a badge.
   Imran was very happy.

Unit 13: The lion and the mouse
Question types: 3 literal, 5 inferential
1. a lion and a mouse.
2. a lion.
3. tickled.
4. harm.
5. the mouse was too small to help a big lion.
6. to set the lion free.
7. hurt.
8. 3, 1, 2, 4:
   The lion woke up.
   The lion caught the mouse.
   The lion was trapped.
   The lion was free.

Unit 14: The classroom
Question types: 1 literal, 5 inferential
1. The labels should be joined to the correct objects in the picture.
2. The labels are computer, window, door, chair and table and should match the objects in the picture.
3. The label 'book' should be placed near to a drawing of a book.
4. tidy.
5. cleaning.
6. wall.

Unit 15: Making a leaf print
Question types: 2 literal, 2 inferential, 1 deductive
1. make a leaf print.
2. The correct order for the sentences is 4, 2, 1, 3:
   Put a leaf with the flat side down on a sheet of newspaper.
   Cover the leaf with a piece of white paper.
   Rub over the white paper with some coloured chalk or a wax crayon.
   Show your leaf print to your friend.

Section 2 *cont.*

3. In any order: a) a leaf b) white paper
   c) chalk or wax crayon d) newspaper.
4. pencil.
5. summer.

Unit 16: Making a badge
Question types: 2 literal, 4 inferential
1. card.
2. Happy Birthday.
3. Velcro.
4. back.
5. a circle.
6. The things you need to make a badge are:
   a shape to draw round, card, scissors, pencil,
   crayons or felt-tipped pens, Velcro, glue.

Unit 17: Banana and marshmallow cheesecake
Queston types: 3 literal, 4 inferential, 1 evaluative
1. to crush the biscuits.
2. sugar and melted butter.
3. the base.
4. chocolate flakes.
5. make it firm.
6. sweet.
7. a knife or scissors.
8. like bananas.

Unit 18: What melts?
Question types: 1 literal, 4 inferential, 1 deductive
1. In any order: a) lolly stick b) bowl
   c) wrapper d) toast
2. Tick: a candle, an ice cube, a snowman, soap
   Cross: an ice-cream cone, a candlestick, a bath
   sponge, pebbles.
3. they get warm.
4. water.
5. burns.
6. A snowman will melt but a scarf doesn't.

Unit 19: The king of beasts
Question types: 4 literal, 3 inferential
1. It is a yellow colour.
2. hard to see in the desert.
3. cat family.
4. climb trees.
5. when it is dark.
6. hot and sunny.
7. The following sentences should be ticked:
   A male lion has strong legs.
   A male lion has a big mane.
   A male lion has a tuft at the end of its tail.

Unit 20: How many teeth?
Question types: 4 literal, 4 inferential
1. when it is six months old.
2. 20 teeth.
3. front.
4. chew.
5. easier.
6. front.
7. first.
8. will get holes in them.

Unit 21: Kavita Brahmbhatt
Question types: 5 literal, 2 inferential
1. cannot hear.
2. hands.
3. They use special signs.
4. telling her mother what to do.
5. she cannot see.
6. a national bravery award.
7. she can hear and see.

Unit 22: Keeping warm
Question types: 2 literal, 3 inferential
1. a sheep's woolly coat.
2. in the winter.
3. a jumper.
4. The correct order for the sentences is 3, 2, 1, 4:
   The fleece is shaved off the sheep.
   The fleece is washed and combed.
   The fleece is spun into wool.
   The wool is used to make things to wear.
5. fleece.

Unit 23: Acorns
Question types: 4 literal, 2 inferential
1. an acorn.
2. the seed.
3. eat.
4. falls.
5. acorn.
6. The pictures should be sequenced in the following order:
   acorn on a twig (third picture)
   acorn on the ground (fourth picture)
   small seedling tree (second picture)
   mature oak tree (first picture).

Unit 24: Ladybirds
Question types: 3 literal, 3 inferential
1. Ladybirds belong to the beetle family.
2. Some ladybirds have seven black spots.
3. fly.
4. greenfly.
5. greenfly.
6. gardeners.

Unit 25: Spiders' webs
Question types: 3 literal, 3 inferential, 1 deductive
1. It spins a web.
2. It eats them.
3. the web.
4. in the centre.
5. it would get very hungry.
6. it is hiding.
7. The correct order is 3, 2, 1. The sentences then read:
   First it makes a square shape.
   Next it spins threads across the square.
   Then it spins a sticky thread in circles.

Unit 26: The rainy day
Question types: 2 literal, 2 inferential, 1 deductive
1. at home.
2. It is raining.
3. a box.
4. boring.
5. he found his watch.

Section 2 *cont.*

Unit 27: Oscar's new trainers
Question types: 3 literal, 3 inferential
1. to school.
2. They are too small.
3. take the bus.
4. a shoe shop.
5. size.
6. run fast.

Unit 28: The haircut
Question types: 4 literal, 3 inferential
1. Jimmy.
2. It was curly.
3. the post office.
4. a tractor.
5. sat still.
6. Jimmy.
7. pleased.

Unit 29: A royal visit
Question types: 5 literal, 2 inferential
1. Queen Mab.
2. make a garden.
3. a garden.
4. smooth and fine.
5. rolled.
6. a seed.
7. the garden.

Unit 30: A mouse in the house
Question types: 5 literal, 3 inferential
1. Liam.
2. up high.
3. The cat might try to get it.
4. shells.
5. a fright.
6. under the bed.
7. Gran.
8. eat the cheese.

Section 3

Unit 1: A hibernating hedgehog
Question types: 5 literal, 3 inferential, 1 deductive
1. hibernating.
2. sleeping through the winter.
3. in the spring.
4. set the alarm.
5. autumn.
6. spring and summer.
7. The hedgehog had overslept.
8. The hedgehog had been asleep for about ten months.
9. Martin Honeysett wrote the poem.

Unit 2: The gerbil
Question types: 6 literal, 3 inferential, 1 evaluative
1. sees; hand.
2. a gerbil.
3. the gerbil's paws.

4. poet.
5. trees.
6. kangaroo.
7. the classroom.
8. There is sand on the floor of the gerbil's hutch.
9. The ground would be sandy.
10. Own answer.

Unit 3: The quarrel
Question types: 5 literal, 4 inferential, 1 evaluative
1. strong; along.
2. slight; night.
3. two.
4. arguing.
5. The quarrelling got worse.
6. the person who wrote the poem.
7. The brother was the first to try to make up the quarrel.
8. Open answer.
9. The person in the poem was right.
10. The person in the poem didn't know what it was about.

Unit 4: Monkey tricks
Question types: 4 literal, 3 inferential, 2 deductive, 1 evaluative
1. shines; knees.
2. in the jungle.
3. swings.
4. she can hear the drums beat.
5. bends her knees.
6. The trees grow close together.
7. He says this because the monkey's nose looks like a coconut.
8. Someone must be beating the drums the monkey can hear.
9. Open answer.
10. Deep in the jungle; see the Mighty Monkey.

Unit 5: Motor cars
Question types: 5 literal, 5 inferential
1. by; track; all; alone; light.
2. shiny.
3. black.
4. in the evening.
5. a flat.
6. in the city.
7. the cars.
8. The flat is high up in the building.
9. The cars are moving slowly.
10. The golden feelers are the lights of the cars.

Unit 6: Finders keepers
Question types: 4 literal, 4 inferential, 2 evaluative
1. no.
2. in the kitchen.
3. a carrot.
4. The person who lost the rabbit will be crying.
5. smooth.
6. wet.
7. She was away with the children from her school.
8. He will try to find out where the rabbit has come from.
9. Open answer.
10. Open answer.

Section ③ *cont.*

Unit 7: The beech tree
Question types: 4 literal, 6 inferential
1. taking a walk.
2. the beech tree.
3. so that he could climb the tree.
4. climb the tree.
5. 30 pence.
6. quickly.
7. Rabbit's grandmother is mentioned in the story.
8. There was a ladder in Grandmother's garden.
9. He planned to climb the ladder.
10. Goat, Tortoise and Puppy didn't agree that Rabbit should use a ladder.

Unit 8: Captain Daylight
Question types: 6 literal, 2 inferential, 1 deductive, 2 evaluative
1. a highwayman.
2. small and round.
3. a robber.
4. carriage pulled by a horse.
5. tell jokes.
6. friend.
7. He tried to rob the passengers on the stagecoach.
8. He was too friendly.
9. Joe had heard all Captain Daylight's jokes.
10. He decided to look frightening.
11. Open answer.

Unit 9: Geraldine gets lucky
Question types: 9 literal, 2 inferential
1. a frog.
2. in a pond.
3. false.
4. thin.
5. marry.
6. a fairy tale.
7. A prince would kiss her.
8. They thought Geraldine was silly to believe the fairy tale.
9. Geraldine's mother didn't think it was funny.
10. A frog can jump ten times its own length.
11. She thought they looked terrible.

Unit 10: Emily and the egg
Question types: 6 literal, 3 inferential, 1 deductive, 1 evaluative
1. in the park.
2. It was enormous.
3. She didn't want her brother to get it.
4. in the garden shed.
5. hatched.
6. The smoke was coming from the dragon.
7. She had seen pictures in story-books.
8. It had a green scaly body with spiky wings and a long, curly tail.
9. She spoke to it softly and gave it some chocolate buttons.
10. The dragon's tongue was hot because they breathe fire.
11. Open answer.

Unit 11: Why hares have long ears
Question types: 6 literal, 4 inferential, 1 evaluative
1. why hares have long ears.
2. build a house.
3. in the forest.
4. knock down the tree.
5. didn't believe.
6. The hare thought that trees were knocked down by running into them with your head.
7. The hare's head went right back into his shoulders.
8. The goat had to get the hare's head out of his shoulders.
9. He had horns on his head.
10. Open answer.
11. When the goat pulled the hare by his ears they were stretched.

Unit 12: Coconut meringues
Question types: 3 literal, 6 inferential, 1 deductive
1. The correct order is:
   1 Whip the egg whites.
   2 Fold in the sugar and coconut.
   3 Put half the mixture into another bowl and colour it with the food colouring.
   4 Pile the mixture in very small heaps on a baking tray.
   5 Bake for 35 minutes.
   6 Remove the tray from the oven.
2. scales.
3. rice.
4. eaten.
5. 11.05am.
6. what you do.
7. The baking tray will be very hot.
8. You would need 250g.
9. You need two bowls so that you can colour half the mixture pink.
10. You would use a whisk.

Unit 13: Which way?
Question types: 4 literal, 4 inferential, 2 deductive
1. The correct order is:
   1 First, go down this road until you come to the post office on your left.
   2 Turn right just after the post office.
   3 Go about 300 metres along the road until you come to the church, which will be on your right.
   4 Turn left down the road opposite the church towards the village hall.
   5 The surgery is next to the village hall. You will see the sign.
2. The woman could live nearby.
3. He should look out for the post office.
4. He must turn right just after the post office.
5. The road leads to the surgery and the village hall.
6. He may be going to see the doctor.
7. He could ask the policeman.
8. The man had to look out for the post office, the church and the village hall.
9. He will see a sign.
10. Go up the road to the church.
    Turn right at the church.
    Go about 300 metres to the end of the road opposite the post office.
    Turn left at the post office.
    Go up the road to the bus stop.

Section 3 *cont.*

Unit 14: Going fishing
Question types: 6 literal, 4 inferential, 1 deductive
1. a tackle shop.
2. wearing layers of clothing.
3. have a rod licence.
4. licence   hook disgorger
   rod   food
   reel   a drink
   bait   waterproof clothes.
5. Bright colours frighten the fish.
6. You may catch the fish they would have caught or frighten them away.
7. The fish may feel the vibrations and swim away.
8. It is better to fish with the sun in front of you so your shadow isn't on the water.
9. You should leave the countryside clean for other people.
10. You need bait to catch the fish with.
11. Bright colours, shadows, vibrations and sudden movements are all things which could frighten the fish.

Unit 15: School news
Question types: 6 literal, 3 inferential, 1 evaluative
1. at the beginning of the autumn term.
2. markings for games.
3. Madame Dupuis.
4. at the end of term.
5. Wednesday.
6. They must send a note to school.
7. She is making a list of children who would like music lessons.
8. You should give your name to your teacher.
9. Both clubs are held on the same night.
10. Open answer.

Unit 16: Newspaper story
Question types: 6 literal, 2 inferential, 2 deductive, 1 evaluative
1. local charities.
2. bulbs.
3. winter.
4. a home for sick people.
5. selling baked goods.
6. Jill Penn wrote the report.
7. She found they had lots of ideas for raising money for charity.
8. They are sending money to Children in Need and the local children's hospice.
9. They have thought of taking dogs for walks, shopping for old or ill people and washing cars.
10. The children's teacher will be helping them.
11. Open answer.

Unit 17: A fishing competition
Question types: 4 literal, 5 inferential, 1 deductive
1. a river.
2. cloudy but dry.
3. Jack Spratt.
4. More people.
5. 22 February.
6. The children are not at school on a Saturday.
7. The children took picnic lunches.
8. It means there were plenty of fish in the river.
9. Josh James and Susie Sands won the competition.
10. Jim fell into the river.

Unit 18: Send an e-mail
Question types: 4 literal, 6 inferential, 1 deductive
1. St Simon's School.
2. melted.
3. south-west.
4. Tuesday.
5. every day except Tuesday.
6. The temperature gets warmer.
7. Friday would be the best day.
8. Tuesday is the worst day of weather.
9. Monday, Tuesday and Wednesday mornings had no sunshine.
10. They had been to a glass factory.
11. St Simon's School sent an e-mail to Dunston Primary School.

Unit 19: A missing dog
Question types: 5 literal, 5 inferential
1. a collie dog.
2. 10.30 at night.
3. Dunston.
4. 31 East Street, Ragford.
5. Bracken.
6. The dog may not know her way round Ragford.
7. The dog may have gone into a shed or garage and got shut in.
8. They might be concerned, and there is a reward offered for finding the dog.
9. The owner's address is on the dog's collar.
10. They could call the dog's name.

Unit 20: Highwayman Dick Turpin
Question types: 6 literal, 4 inferential
1. in Essex.
2. a butcher.
3. thirty-three.
4. stealing cattle.
5. accidentally shot.
6. He earned his living by robbing people.
7. They robbed lonely farmhouses.
8. You could read about them in the London Evening Post.
9. The Essex Gang were thieves.
10. Dick hanged himself.

Unit 21: Mary Anning
Question types: 8 literal, 1 inferential
1. 1799.
2. 12.
3. in a seaside town.
4. fossil.
5. she could be hit by falling rocks from the cliff.
6. She sold her fossils.
7. She was the first person to find an ichthyosaur fossil.
8. A pterodactylus was a flying reptile.
9. Famous scientists came to Mary's shop.

Section 3 *cont.*

Unit 22: Greyfriar's Bobby
Question types: 8 literal, 3 inferential
1. in Edinburgh.
2. a dog.
3. faithfulness.
4. master.
5. guard the cattle.
6. Mrs Ramsay gave Bobby and his master breakfast.
7. He stayed near Old Jock's gravestone.
8. He stayed near his master for 14 years.
9. Mrs Ramsay fed Bobby every day.
10. Baroness Burdett Coutts had a statue made.
11. The statue stands outside Greyfriar's churchyard gates.

Unit 23: Eggs for tea
Question types: 3 literal, 4 inferential, 2 deductive, 1 evaluative
1. through the shell.
2. The eggs are fresh.
3. flock.
4. protein; vitamins; minerals.
5. People who keep their own hens would not need to buy eggs from a shop.
6. A chick needs air when it is hatching.
7. Different ways to cook an egg are boiled; poached; fried; scrambled; as an omelette.
8. Open answer.
9. Eggs can be used to make cakes, puddings and sauces.
10. See diagram below.

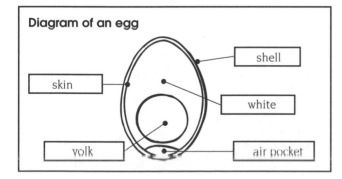

Diagram of an egg

Unit 24: Hedgehogs
Question types: 7 literal, 3 inferential, 1 deductive
1. It has prickles.
2. not very good.
3. is awake at night.
4. swimming; smelling; climbing.
5. Answers should include four of the following:
   snails   berries
   slugs   nuts
   worms   eggs
6. The hedgehog sniffs out its food.
7. It sleeps all winter.
8. There is not enough food for them to eat in winter.
9. They are very prickly.
10. The babies are called piglets. They are born in May or June.
11. You might hear a hedgehog snoring.

Unit 25: Coconuts
Question types: 7 literal, 3 inferential, 1 deductive
1. Portuguese sailors.
2. in India.
3. grinning face.
4. on palm trees.
5. language.
6. It comes from India.
7. The name is kalpa vriksha.
8. They are green.
9. It is made from the coarse fibres inside the coconut case.
10. You would have to crack it open.
11. See diagram below.

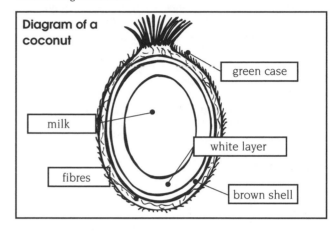

Diagram of a coconut

green case
milk
white layer
fibres
brown shell

Unit 26: Are you what you eat?
Question types: 8 literal, 2 inferential
1. what you usually eat.
2. eating something of everything.
3. do not eat meat.
4. protein.
5. apple; rice pudding; carrot.
6. It is wrong to kill animals for food; for religious reasons; it is a healthier diet.
7. They say that their teeth are for eating meat.
8. Meat has protein and vitamins.
9. They ate Early man and each other.
10. We need protein to build up muscles, bones and other parts of the body.

Unit 27: Getting to school
Question types: 7 literal, 1 inferential, 2 deductive, 1 evaluative
1. the environment.
2. They could walk to work.
3. to make dirty.
4. It is safe. It helps children to make friends.
5. The list should include:
   walk   cycle
   bus   train
6. The car engines pollute the air.
7. The roads are dangerous.
8. They might spend an hour.
9. The roads are narrow and there may not be any footpaths.
10. It is dangerous to cross busy roads.
11. Open answer.

Section ③ cont.

Unit 28: Mobile phones
Question types: 5 literal, 4 inferential, 1 deductive
1. when they ring in class.
2. true.
3. depend.
4. parents.
5. They think they will be safer,
6. I could phone home and ask someone to bring it to school.
7. They could find it a nuisance when children keep phoning for no reason.
8. Mobile phones are most useful when there is an emergency.
9. They use a telephone box.
10. You can use them almost anywhere.

Unit 29: What happened to the dinosaurs?
Question types: 7 literal, 3 inferential, 1 evaluative
1. millions.
2. all over the world.
3. idea.
4. other dinosaurs.
5. rock from space.
6. The plants could stop growing.
7. A cloud of dust would have made the Earth dark and cold.
8. Water vapour could have trapped the heat of the Sun.
9. Dust and gas blocked out the sunshine.
10. They can tell from fossils.
11. Open answer.

Unit 30: Miss Muffet's new friend
Question types: 4 literal, 5 inferential, 1 evaluative
1. a spider.
2. making cheese.
3. stool.
4. a reporter.
5. Miss Muffet screamed and upset her curds and whey.
6. He was hit on the nose by the tuffet.
7. He wanted some curds and whey.
8. She felt sorry for him.
9. Open answer.
10. It will eat them.

Unit 31: Emergency 999
Question types: 5 literal, 4 inferential, 1 evaluative
1. three.
2. to school.
3. from the alleyway.
4. She saw a leg.
5. She was pushed over and robbed.
6. The boys live in the same street as Mrs Green.
7. Mrs Green thought she had a broken leg.
8. Aylesha had a mobile phone.
9. It was morning.
10. Open answer.

Unit 32: The goose that laid the golden egg
Question types: 5 literal, 3 inferential, 1 deductive, 1 evaluative
1. a cottage in the country.
2. the wife.
3. the egg would make them rich.
4. she wanted a new dress.
5. She could sell the egg.
6. It laid two eggs.
7. They expected to find gold.
8. It was the wife's idea.
9. She found the egg at teatime.
10. Open answer.

Unit 33: The coconut shy
Question types: 5 literal, 5 inferential, 1 evaluative
1. it is carnival time.
2. a stall where you try to knock coconuts off stands for a prize.
3. Mum.
4. coconut milk.
5. whiskery and spotted.
6. He paid £2.
7. He could hear the coconut milk.
8. He will make holes through the dark spots.
9. You can eat the coconut meat.
10. They might use them for food for the birds.
11. Open answer.

Unit 34: The lost rabbit
Question types: 4 literal, 4 inferential, 2 deductive
1. brothers.
2. a group Ben belongs to.
3. lives next door.
4. Ben.
5. Snowy was probably a white rabbit.
6. Ben didn't fasten the cage properly.
7. It had been raining.
8. He looks in the neighbours' gardens and puts up a notice in the shop.
9. A girl in the next street found Snowy.
10. He said Snowy could get eaten.

Unit 35: King Midas
Question types: 4 literal, 6 inferential, 2 evaluative
1. a king and a Greek god.
2. more gold.
3. storage room for money.
4. His gold is his favourite thing.
5. greedy.
6. Dionysus was a god.
7. to teach King Midas a lesson.
8. King Midas made Dionysus welcome.
9. Everything King Midas touched would turn to gold.
10. Dionysus did not want to turn into gold.
11. Open answer.
12. Open answer.